FUNDRAISING GUIDES

AFTER THE GRANT

The Nonprofit's Guide to Good Stewardship

Judith B. Margolin, Editor
Elan DiMaio, Assistant Editor
Sumin Lee, Assistant Editor

Acknowledgements

The Foundation Center is indebted to the chapter authors who gave generously of their time and expertise to submit text replete with targeted advice for first-time recipients of foundation grants. We are also grateful to the many grantmakers who participated in interviews and submitted various materials related to their funding policies and procedures. These appear as examples throughout the guide. In particular we would like to thank Marilyn Hoyt for her generous contributions from start to finish. And we would like to thank Elan DiMaio and Sumin Lee for their excellent editorial support and Christine Innamorato for her design and production skills.

Library of Congress Cataloging-in-Publication Data

After the grant / Judith B. Margolin, editor.
    p. cm. — (Fundraising guides)
  Includes bibliographical references and index.
  ISBN 978-1-59542-301-6 (pbk. : alk. paper) 1. Endowments—United States.
2. Research grants--United States. I. Margolin, Judith B. II. Foundation Center.
  HV41.9.U5A36 2010
  658.15'224--dc22

                          2010000817

Table of Contents

Foreword

Years ago, when working as a foundation program officer, I remember successfully defending my idea for a bold, new strategy. Afterwards, while walking out of the President's office, the foundation's Vice President leaned over and said: "Now you're in trouble, she likes your idea." That was his wry way of saying that the real work had only just begun.

That sentiment captures the theme of this book. So much of the philanthropy "business" is focused on getting or making a grant. Nonprofits diligently research prospects and struggle to capture their dreams in the endless formats for grant proposals, which foundations then scrutinize and follow-up with lots of questions. If all goes well at the end of the process the foundation's Trustees give their nod and out pops a grant.

Success? Yes, up to a point. Getting a grant is cause for celebration at any nonprofit and for a foundation it is the culmination of a lengthy process of due diligence and one step further in meeting the payout requirement. But the real work—turning the aspirations contained in a proposal into accomplishments that can be described, measured, analyzed, and communicated—has only just begun.

At the Foundation Center, we like to teach that getting a grant begins with a relationship. The authors in this book describe the many ways in which that relationship between a nonprofit and a foundation grows and matures through signing grant letters, expressing gratitude, filing reports, communicating the inevitable course corrections that arise in the course of a project, and more.

Through the grant, nonprofits and foundations set out on a journey together. This book gives you the roadmap.

Brad Smith
President
The Foundation Center

Introduction

"Congratulations, you got a grant!" These words are music to most nonprofit executives' ears. Several chapters in this book, in fact, begin with a variation on this theme. The fact that congratulations are in order usually implies something important that has reached a successful conclusion. Yet this guide is based on the premise that receipt of grant funds is just the beginning. Often a grant from a foundation, if managed properly, can lead to a long and fruitful relationship with that funder and perhaps with others as well. But managing the relationship effectively includes a series of essential steps.

First is receipt of the grant and being sure you have a full understanding of all the implications of accepting this funding. The next critical step is acknowledgement of the grant and completion of all the necessary paperwork. This is followed by establishing internal systems to enable your organization to expend, monitor, and account for the grant funds. Along the way there will be meetings with your funder, interim updates, and a variety of communications and interactions by phone, by e-mail, or in person, including inviting your funder to various events held by your organization. At the end of the grant period you will need to be in a position to report back to the funder in detail not only about how the money was spent, but about precisely what results you achieved, what was learned, and what the implications are for the future. And then (and this is not the "final" step, because you hope it will lead to more funding), there is the request for renewal support for this or some other project run by your organization. All of these steps relate to "stewardship" of foundation grant funds, and that is the subject of this guide.

The various chapters in this guide cover all of the topics mentioned above in a fairly straightforward manner in the sequence just provided. So when you read this guide, you will find Chapter 1: The Funded Proposal, Chapter 2: The Grant Award Letter, Chapter 3: Managing the Grant Project, etc. Exceptions to this chronology are the topics of communication and, specifically, meetings with funders, which can and do take place at any and every point during the grant cycle. Since such interactions are so critical to the grantmaker/grantee relationship, both of these topics are touched on in one way or another in most chapters. But they also have separate chapters devoted to them. If you are a first-time grantee, as with any new relationship, there are sure to be roadblocks that crop up along the way. In Appendix A we have provided a "Troubleshooting Guide," in question-and-answer format, where an experienced fundraiser who has seen it all provides practical advice about how to respond when relations with your funder do not go as smoothly as you might like. We have also provided a bibliography for further investigation of many of the topics covered here. You can read the guide from beginning to end, or you can home in on just those chapters that interest you, since each is written by a different author. Finally, we have provided an index so that you can look up particular topics that are covered in multiple chapters.

The Foundation Center's print publications include a number of guides that have proven essential to managers of the nation's nonprofits, as well as books to which grantmakers have contributed that are of particular interest to grantseekers: *Foundation Fundamentals, The Foundation Center's Guide to Proposal Writing*, and *The Grantseeker's Guide to Winning Proposals*. These guides focus on what those new to the grantseeking process need to understand about foundations, how they operate, what resources are available to help identify and approach funding prospects that best match a nonprofit's requirements, and how to craft a compelling grant proposal and budget.

With increasing frequency, however, those who come to the Center's libraries and Cooperating Collections; take our free classes, webinars, and full-day seminars; and visit our web site and utilize the "Ask Us" service to query our online librarians have begun requesting a different type of guide—one that could assist them in effectively managing grant funds once received. First-time grantees require advice about developing a productive relationship with their funders and how to position themselves for further grant funding in the future. These requests from members of the Center's nonprofit audience coincide with an increasing emphasis on the part of foundation boards on determining the impact of their own grantmaking while at the same time ensuring that grant funds awarded are being used as intended. Meanwhile, a challenging economic climate makes the processes of both applying for and awarding grant funds ever more competitive, with the very future of many nonprofits dependent on navigating these waters successfully.

For all of these reasons and, since—despite a critical need for such a guide—very little has been written on the topic of what should happen *after* a grant is awarded, the Foundation Center decided to compile this new publication. To secure the best possible advice, we reached out to our friends and colleagues in the philanthropic community, being sure to include those on both sides of the grantmaker/grantseeker equation. We are most grateful to our chapter authors, who represent both foundation executives and veteran fundraisers (and one or two who have worn both hats), and who generously gave of their time and expertise to share their hard-won knowledge with our readers. Brief biographies of the chapter authors will be found in Appendix B. Many other grantmakers contributed to the guide as well, by submitting sample documents for use as illustrations in the various chapters or by agreeing to be interviewed by our chapter authors and Foundation Center staff. Their examples and quotes from these interviews will be found throughout the guide. We also sought out recommendations from colleagues in the field as to exemplary grant projects where management of the grantmaker/grantee relationship was critical to success. We uncovered three such model grants, and these are described in detail in Chapter 10: The Successful Grant. We especially want to thank these three funders and the three grantees for their excellent stewardship of foundation funds and for their guidance in helping us compile the case studies you will find in this chapter.

It is our sincere hope and expectation that this guide will fill a void in the practical literature related to grantsmanship, and that it will serve both as a truly useful tool to those new to the process and as a reminder of best practices to those who have been involved in philanthropy for many years. We expect that novice and veteran fundraisers as well as foundation program officers and trustees will find it of great interest. Here's to good stewardship!

Judith B. Margolin
Editor

The Funded Proposal

Victoria Kovar

By definition, foundations hold their funds in the public trust. All foundations, like all other nonprofit organizations, have a mission to provide betterment to the community. However, very few, if any, foundations are able to achieve their mission solely through their own programs, and so rely on grantmaking to organizations to turn that grant support into action. Children are nurtured and educated, the hungry are fed, the environment is protected, broken spirits are made whole, and artistic visions are realized with the help of grant support.

There are many reasons that compel a foundation to give—an exciting idea, an urgent community need, a great opportunity for change, or a commitment to sustain the ongoing work of an agency. Regardless of the reason, a grant indicates the belief that the funded project will help fulfill the foundation's own mission. As you exist to serve the community, we exist to serve you. But even the largest foundation is unable to fulfill every request received, so we must make choices on which to fund and which to decline.

As more attention is paid to professional philanthropy and as regulations increase, there is also an increased expectation for the careful stewardship of foundation funds. This includes following best management practices and also choosing the most worthy recipients for these limited resources. The formal proposal is the most reliable and consistent way to sort through the competing requests.

The proposal serves many functions for the funder. It provides education on social needs and the context in which those needs will be met by the proposed solution. It may introduce the organization to the funder, or update the funder on changes at a known organization. It provides a way for the funder to evaluate the organization as a whole and to determine the agency's capacity to carry out the work proposed.

The best proposal is clear, complete, and to the point. The best proposal:

- Describes the need to be met and lays out a plan to meet it.

- Identifies key individuals responsible for the work.

- Includes a budget that is complete, detailed, and accurate.

- Explains how the agency will measure results.

- Uses simple, concise, and declarative statements explaining why the project, program, or organizational function is central to the agency's mission and priorities.

- Provides all the information necessary for the funder to make the final decision.

Keep in mind that your funder is most likely processing many other applications as well as yours and has limited time to thoroughly review and move the applications through its funding process. Your proposal should be easy to read, both in the language used and in its visual presentation. Break up your narrative into small paragraphs, and consider using bullets, lists, or charts to organize complicated information.

Follow the funder's directions closely. Make sure you thoroughly read grant guidelines, application forms, and any other documentation from the foundation that details procedures or requirements. Provide only the information that is relevant to each section in the application form without repetition or overlap. Simple things, like restating the headings or numbering from the application, make a big difference. The application form is designed to conform to the foundation's review process and any diversion from that can hinder the process.

Check your proposal for accuracy, and proofread the entire document before sending it. You might be surprised at how many proposals have incomplete sections, unfinished sentences, incorrect math, or mistakenly identified funders. These are not usually fatal flaws, but any amount of time the funder spends on correcting a proposal's small errors is time that would be better spent engaging in your ideas and goals.

The advice foundations often give to an applicant in preparation for a grant proposal is to write it with the assumption that the funder knows nothing about the project or the agency. Even if you have a history with the funder, the funder might have new staff or board members who are unfamiliar with that history. Ask someone who has no connection to the project to read the application. If that person finds it clear, convincing, and easy to understand, then your funder will as well.

Foundations and other funders may have application forms that are specific to their grantmaking process, but they generally want to know the same basic information. The following is a detailed description of the major components of a proposal, what each should include, and how the funder uses them.

Contact information

This is the simplest part, but still requires attention. Your organization's legal name, address, and contact information should be clear and complete. If you use a post office box for correspondence, be sure to include your physical address as well.

Depending on the project and the funder, you may have the chief executive, a board officer, or a development or program staff person listed as the contact for the grant. Make sure the right person is assigned. The contact person should have comprehensive knowledge of the program and the grant application to be able to respond to questions the funder may have. If there is a more appropriate person to contact about the project as it goes forward, or to answer specific technical questions, let the funder know and make introductions as necessary.

Organizational background

This includes your mission statement, history, and a summary of your organization's work and achievements. This is an opportunity to show why your organization is uniquely qualified to do this work. Be complete in your description, even if your organization has received funding in the past, but remember to keep it concise and relevant. Think of this as the written equivalent to a one-minute "elevator speech" about your organization. Do not use this section to explain the specific project or program for which you seek funding. Foundation staff may use this section to provide a broad overview of your agency to the decision makers, and it can be frustrating to have to edit the information for that purpose.

Project description

This section introduces your program or purpose to the funder. It should give the funder an overview of the key points in the proposal and why this work is important. It can explain how your program or organization meets the funder's grant criteria and priorities. The project description is a summary, so brevity and clarity are important. It gives the funder a general understanding of the project and prepares the funder for the detailed information to follow.

Statement of need

The proposal should define the problem or opportunity that is addressed by the project. Explain the need, the social or environmental factors that contribute to it, and the scope of the need within the community. You need to provide credible evidence to support your analysis, which may be from your own program data, outside research and statistics, or both. Be careful to summarize this information without bogging the narrative down with data.

Anticipated effect

Explain what you want to accomplish and how you will define success. You should state the expected outcome of the project, and how the work you do will affect that outcome. Funders are looking for clear, measurable objectives that directly relate to your statement of need and your stated goals.

Population served

Identify the audience served by the program. Be as specific as possible. Even if your project is free and open to the public, you will not likely serve everyone in the community. You may use general demographic information to establish the broad societal context, but be specific about who is directly served by your work. How many people will you serve? Funders like hard numbers. How will you identify them and how will they find you? How will you track who has been served? Whether your program or service is provided to many individuals one time or to a few individuals multiple times, be clear and explicit in how you are calculating those numbers.

Work plan and activities

This identifies the process by which you will meet your objectives and accomplish your goals. Include a detailed description of the activities involved, where and when they will occur, and who will carry them out. The work plan should contain activities of sufficient scope and intensity to reach the desired outcome. They should be concrete, realistic, and achievable. You should include a timeline with a distinct beginning and end, even if the program or function is ongoing.

Logic models

A logic model is a graphic and sequential representation of how the organization will carry out the work proposed. It illustrates the relationship between the resources (inputs), process (action and activities), service delivery (outputs), and results (outcomes) of the project. A logic model is an effective tool in planning, implementing, and evaluating a project. Depending on the funder, there are variations of the logic model that may be required. Most funders that require it will offer guidelines and resources for developing a logic model.

Request amount

Unless otherwise instructed, the size of your grant request should be typical of the funder's average grant amount, and should reflect the costs you have identified in the proposal budget. Funders usually have a range of amounts that they consider appropriate, which may vary depending on the size of the project or the organization. You can get a good feel for what amount is appropriate by reviewing other grants made by the funder, which may be listed on the funder's web site or in an annual report. If you are still unsure, ask for guidance.

Proposal budget

Simply put, this tells the funder how much the project will cost and how you will pay for it. The proposal budget should include all the direct costs for the project or program. These can include staff costs, materials, equipment, travel, printing, postage, publicity, and supplies for program participants. Staff costs should include salary as well as taxes and fringe benefits. You should also estimate overhead costs—usually administrative and operational costs for the organization that are allocated across the programs or functions of your agency. It is important that these be accurate estimates that are supported by your operating budget and financial reports. Some funders may have specific guidelines, rules, or restrictions on funding overhead expenses. You should follow these precisely.

Cost is only half the story. Many funders want detailed information on the income that will support this project in addition to the amount you have requested. You should include income that is already committed from your own resources or other outside funding, as well as pending applications or requests to other funders or donors. Earned income and in-kind donations should be clearly identified. A good budget will include income sufficient to cover the project's expenses. A negative balance can be a red flag to the funder that the agency's planning is inadequate.

Depending on the funder, the proposal budget may be of your own design or formatted to a template or form specified by the application requirements. When it comes time to report, you will likely have to submit a statement comparing the proposal budget to the actual income and expenses. It is important to keep track of the budget in a way that will allow you to easily compare what happened with what was proposed. Be sure that the person who is responsible for reporting fully understands the budget, or has access to other personnel with that knowledge.

Fundraising plan

It is rare for a funder to support a program or project in its entirety, so funders may want to know the plan for funding the project now and in the future. New projects, especially, require a thoughtful and realistic development plan that explains how the work will be sustained beyond the term of the grant. "We will continue to raise funds" or "We will write more grants" are unsatisfactory answers. A good fundraising plan includes a variety of funding sources and mechanisms. Diversity in funding sources is a characteristic of strong, stable nonprofit organizations, demonstrating broad community support for your work. Every donation and grant from other funders acts as an endorsement for your organization.

Partnerships and collaborations

No organization works in a vacuum, and funders like to see how an agency and program interact with others in the area of need. Most organizations work with other agencies or partners in some way to help them achieve their missions. This can range from casual associations like professional affiliations or networking, to more specific connections such as client referrals, to formalized collaborations with each participant contributing an essential function suited to his or her expertise. If partnerships with other agencies play an important role in the project or the delivery of services, be sure to include this information. You might want to include a letter of recommendation from partners with whom you work closely.

Evaluation plan

For the funder, the evaluation plan provides a good indicator of organizational capacity, since it explains how the grantee will evaluate its own work and effectiveness. The evaluation plan is an important part of a strong proposal, as this provides the information necessary to make a full and accurate report to the funder when the grant term or project is completed. A complete and clear evaluation plan is especially important if the grantee has an opportunity for continued funding for the project in the future.

Most funders require some kind of reporting, and many have a form specifically for this purpose. The grant recipient should study this form and be familiar with its requirements well in advance of the report deadline. Ideally you will have a chance to review the form, even as you develop your proposal, to be sure you are prepared to gather the information that is needed for the report and build that into the evaluation plan.

The evaluation plan should correspond to the specific components of the proposal, allowing both the organization and the funder to determine if progress was made toward the overall goals and objectives. It can include simple quantitative measurements, such as numbers of people served by a project or the variety of activities that were carried out. It may also include qualitative measurements to determine the outcomes of the project and its effectiveness. The scope of the plan should be proportional to the level of complexity of the funded project or program.

Attachments and organizational documents

Most funders require organizational documents that support the information provided in the proposal. These typically include:

- Operating budget
- Current financial reports
- 990 tax form
- Audited financial statements
- List of the board of directors and their professional affiliations
- IRS determination letter identifying the organization's tax-exempt status
- Annual reports

Other organizational documents may have contributed to the creation of your proposal, such as a mission statement, project data, program evaluations, strategic plan, research reports, and key policies and procedures. Be sure you are familiar with and have access to all of this information, both for your own use and in case your funder has questions. You may not be able to answer every question yourself, but you should know who in your agency can. You should assume that the funder will thoroughly review these documents. For the funder, this provides a way to evaluate the management capacity of the organization. Complete, up-to-date, and well-prepared supporting documentation demonstrates your organization's management capacity. Funders want to support strong, well-managed organizations.

Matching requirements and conditional grants

Some grants are given with contingencies—matching requirements or other conditions that must be met by the agency before funding is received. A common requirement is for the grantee to raise a certain amount of money before the grant is paid—it could be raising the full project budget or an amount to match the grant.

The matching grant serves a useful function for both the organization and the funder. For the organization, it provides an important endorsement, an incentive for others to give, and a way to leverage the grant to gather more support. For the funder, it ensures that the organization has a commitment to the project and the ability to secure the resources necessary to carry it out.

Other conditions may include confirmation of partnerships or permissions, the submission of an agency's development plan or strategic plan, hiring a specific staff position, or other pending action related to the funded project. It is important that you understand the nature of the contingency or conditions of the matching requirement, and the deadlines for meeting those requirements. If something is unclear you should feel free to contact the funder to seek clarification.

Grant contracts or agreements

Many funders utilize formal grant contracts or agreements with their grantees. The contract may specify the use of the funding, the grant term, payment schedule, reporting deadlines and requirements, and other conditions of the grant. It is important that you fully understand the contract and adhere to its provisions.

Reporting

Carefully note the deadlines required and use the appropriate form, if provided. If you cannot meet the deadline, contact the funder right away with an explanation of the reason for the delay. Even if your project falls short of expectations or fails, it is important that you make an honest, forthright report. Some of the best reports we have received were for projects that missed the mark. The reports were good because of the valuable lessons learned, and the honesty and accountability shown by the agency. The worst thing you can do is fail to report. This will jeopardize your opportunity to apply for future grants.

Building a relationship with your funder

Relationships start with communication. Before the grant, you may have opportunities to speak with or meet foundation staff in person. Some foundations conduct site visits during the application process to learn more about the project and how the organization works. Ask the funder how you can prepare for the visit and what information the funder would like to review. You may want to invite officers and board members to a meeting with funders, as well as key program personnel.

Most foundations have small staffs, so you may not be able to meet in person, but they might welcome e-mails or phone conversations. Be sure to ask about the foundation's preferences for communication. If they do not have time to meet or consult with applicants, they will tell you so; but you won't know unless you ask. The funder may be happy to talk about the foundation's guidelines and how your proposal can meet those guidelines, and give you good advice as you prepare your application.

After the grant, your communication with the funder has a significant impact on your developing relationship, informing their perception of your organization and their willingness to make another grant in the future.

Be sure to thank the funder after the grant is approved, as it is a celebratory occasion for both of you. A hand-written note is appreciated. Let your board and staff know about the grant, and publicize the information if that is something the funder encourages. Many funders like to have their good work known in the community. On the other hand, your funder probably does not want a plaque. Spend your limited resources on your program, not on the foundation.

Communicate your successes. Let the funder know when other funds have been received for the project, or when you receive key endorsements or recognition for your program or organization. Remember that your success is one way that funders measure their success.

Communicate your challenges. Notify the funder right away if there are substantive changes to the funded program. This could be changes in staffing, changes in partnerships, budget adjustments, or previously unidentified needs that impact the project. Do not be afraid to speak honestly with the funder about your challenges or the changes to work through. However, make sure that you also discuss the agency's plan of action to address the changing needs. Be prepared to send revised documents or other updates to the funders in writing for their records. Funders generally do not expect everything to go exactly as planned, especially for new or pilot programs. They do need to be reassured that their funds are managed well and will be used in a way that is consistent with what was approved.

Provide learning opportunities. Ask if the funder would like to be added to your mailing list, to receive program updates or publicity materials. Invite the funder to meetings, workshops, or other activities of the funded program. Funders often like to see the plan in action.

Always refer back to the proposal and make sure that your communication is consistent with the information in it. The proposal is a roadmap for the funder. Whatever the final destination, the proposal is the primary resource that influences the funder's decision to support you on your journey. If you need to provide additional information to what was included in the proposal, be sure to send it. Remember to keep information concise, easy to read, and relevant to the proposal.

Your successful implementation of the program and management of the grant funds has a huge influence on the likelihood of receiving future funding, but the relationship with a funder has many more benefits than just money. Funders can be your organization's champion and, by their support, encourage others to give. They can make introductions and connections with other funders, organizations, and community leaders. They can offer strategic advice in planning of future projects.

Your grant is not a gift in the traditional sense. It is not a favor. It is an investment. Foundations tend to think in terms of investment and many have a long-term outlook. Many foundations have grant files from decades past and those records show the long-term value of investments by the foundation in young agencies that would prove to become invaluable community institutions.

Building these relationships with funders is not always easy—like any others, they require cultivation, care, and good faith. Some of our long-term relationships have had rocky periods to work through, and some have become more or less close as projects and priorities change over time. All of our good relationships are marked by open communication, honesty, and trust. Whether this is your first grant from a funder or your twentieth, the funded proposal formalizes this relationship into a partnership between your organization and your funder to benefit the community.

What follows is a full proposal for support for a peer mentoring program submitted on the Lincoln/Lancaster County Grantmakers Common Application Form to the Cooper Foundation by Nebraska Community Foundation. The program subsequently received funding from the Cooper Foundation. This is an excellent example of a proposal that incorporates the advice provided in this chapter.

Lincoln/Lancaster County Grantmakers
Common Application Form
(02/20/2007)

◆━━━◆

Foundation Applied To: **The Cooper Foundation**

Application Date: **March 5, 2008**

Organization's Federal Tax I.D. Number: **47-0769903**

I. ORGANIZATIONAL INFORMATION
Provide the following information in two pages using this format.

A. Organization Name   <u>Nebraska Community Foundation</u>
      (List fiscal agent for collaborations)

B. Address/9-digit Zip Code <u>650 J St. Ste. 305,</u>
           <u>PO Box 83107, Lincoln, NE 68501-3107</u>

C. Website   <u>www.nebcommfound.org</u>

D. Chief Executive Officer   Jeffrey G Yost

     D.1. Telephone number   <u>402-323-7330</u>   D.2. Fax <u>402-323-7349</u>

     D.3. Email address   <u>jeffyost@nebcommfound.org</u>

E. Contact Person and Title   _____
                       (If other than the Chief Executive)

     E.1. Telephone number   _____E.2. Fax _____

     E.3. Email address   _____

F. **Purpose of Request**
    A brief summary of the amount requested and its purpose. Limit it to this space.

The Nebraska Community Foundation requests funding support to implement a peer mentoring program for our affiliated fund leaders. NCF receives far more requests from affiliated fund leaders for training, education and on-site coaching than it has resources to provide. Over the past 15 years, a number of fund leaders have become fully committed to our mission of rural capacity building through philanthropy. They have gained valuable experience and knowledge, which they are eager to share and reciprocate. We are developing a strategy to increase and formalize peer-to-peer mentoring, which will augment and extend the hands-on training provided by our development staff and reinforce our grassroots approach. Peer influence and mentoring has led to several affiliated funds moving to the next level of effectiveness and success. With only three development staff members available for on-site assistance, we view peer mentoring as a critically important strategy for providing high-level, value-added services and achieving our mission.

_____   _____
(Signature of Chairperson of the Board)   **(Signature of the Chief Executive Officer)**

Lincoln/Lancaster County Grantmakers
Common Application Form (02/20/2007)

II. PROPOSAL NARRATIVE: <u>10 Pages Maximum. Clarity and brevity are encouraged.</u>

A. FUNDING REQUEST
1. Amount Requested: **$20,000 per year for three years**
2. Objective................**State the objective(s) and the underlying need, problem or opportunity.**

The Nebraska Community Foundation requests funding support to develop and implement a peer mentoring program for our affiliated fund leaders. The Nebraska Community Foundation provides financial management, strategic development, education and training, planned giving information and technical assistance to 202 community, organizational and donor advised affiliated funds in 171 communities located in 72 Nebraska counties.

We describe NCF as a community development institution that uses philanthropy as a tool. NCF does not make grants itself, rather, we empower local leaders to raise money and make grants for community improvement through their own affiliated funds. As a 501(c)(3) umbrella organization, our primary strategy is to serve as an effective fiduciary agent while building the capacity of local leaders to achieve ambitious community philanthropy goals. Specifically, we encourage local leaders to set the goal of securing through charitable gifts at least five percent of their community's intergenerational wealth transfer in permanent community endowments. Our analysis projects that $94 billion of wealth in rural Nebraska will be transferred from one generation to the next within the next few decades.

Today, 87 of our community-based affiliated funds are actively building endowments to benefit their hometowns. Importantly, these 87 affiliated funds now have over $37 million in endowed assets and confirmed expectancies, more than triple the total five years ago. This success can be attributed in large part to the efforts of NCF's three development staff members hired over a period of time since 2002. To date they have made more than 10,550 contacts with community leaders, donors and financial planners, providing significant assistance to both new and existing community-based affiliated funds.

Currently the demand for training and assistance far exceeds the time and capacity of our NCF development staff. To address this challenge, the Nebraska Community Foundation has a plan to use "mentors" to extend our reach and involvement with community leaders who are learning to become effective champions and advocates for their hometown community foundations. Over the past few years, NCF has witnessed significant measurable outcomes achieved as a result of peer-to-peer sharing of success stories and strategies among local community-based affiliated fund leaders. Through our regional and statewide training sessions and through board involvement with one another and with neighboring communities, opportunities for peer learning and mentoring have evolved both naturally and intentionally.

We are developing a strategy to increase and formalize the level of peer-to-peer mentoring among our affiliated fund leaders, which in turn will help to reinforce and extend the services provided by our development staff. Our plan calls for capitalizing on the energy these relationships are producing by institutionalizing and empowering peer mentors to increase their own capacity while teaching others. Peer mentors will help to augment our development staff efforts and reinforce our grassroots approach.

*3. Population Served...***Include as much information as possible, such as numbers, location, socio-economic status, ethnicity, gender, age, physical ability and language.**

Our target population is located in 171 primarily rural Nebraska communities in 72 counties, which have established affiliated funds through the statewide Nebraska Community Foundation. The population served is entirely reflective of the communities themselves regarding socio-economic status, ethnicity, gender, age, physical ability and language. Approximately 2,000 community leaders serve on local affiliated fund governing boards.

4. *Effect……………...*State the anticipated effect on the need, problem or opportunity.

NCF's peer mentoring program will help our affiliated fund leaders recognize and take action steps to achieve higher levels of performance in key areas for effective community endowment building. NCF describes "thresholds" for high-performing affiliated funds as follows:

- Community-wide celebrations are held annually.
- 80 percent of affiliated fund advisory committee members are actively making donor visitations.
- 80 percent of grant making dollars are strategically invested in long-term community benefits.
- 100 percent of fund committee members make annual contributions.
- The number of new donors increases by 20 percent annually.
- The action plan is reviewed monthly and revised quarterly.
- Committee meetings are held monthly with a 90 percent attendance rate.
- 80 percent of community donors renew or upgrade contributions annually.
- 80 percent of fund advisory committee members have included their fund in their estate plans.
- At least 5 percent of the community's projected 10-year transfer of wealth has been captured as charitable gifts to the community endowment.

Robust community endowments create a stable, predictable source of income for community development and improvement efforts based on locally controlled assets and decision making. Our peer mentors will be experienced leaders of affiliated funds that are achieving these high standards of performance. They have used NCF tools and have been guided by our development staff members to become increasingly proficient in cultivating philanthropy in their own communities. They have invaluable personal experience and lessons to share about grassroots community philanthropy. They are also strong advocates of the NCF system of community endowment building and have developed close relationships with NCF staff and board members.

Peer learning and mentoring have evolved both spontaneously and intentionally through our regional and statewide training opportunities and through networking among affiliated fund leaders from different communities. In McCook, Nebraska, with a population of 7,994, local affiliated fund leaders admit that they were struggling early on to make real progress until they began to talk to leaders from the tiny town of Shickley, Nebraska. With a population of only 376, Shickley has managed to raise nearly $1.8 million in assets, expectancies and pledges for its endowment. By trading stories and strategies, McCook leaders were encouraged to jumpstart their efforts. McCook launched challenge grants, a founders club and began targeted donor visitations for major planned gifts. Today, McCook is among NCF's top three endowment-building communities.

In Nebraska City, fund leaders had planned to build a permanent unrestricted endowment, but the plan had sat on the shelf for 18 months. Then the newly elected chair met members of the Keith County Community Foundation at NCF's Rural Philanthropy Conference. Keith County's success in bringing the community together to build an endowment of $400,000 inspired the Nebraska City board. They dusted off their plan and launched a capital campaign for their endowment. Nebraska City revised its case statement to focus on "investing in people" by supporting entrepreneurs, non-traditional students, leadership development, and especially, youth. They adopted a policy to have 20 percent of their endowment allocated to youth issues and projects, and formed a youth advisory committee, which has proven to be a key component to their fundraising efforts.

These are just two examples of the power of peer learning. There are many more. We must act intentionally to create these opportunities on a much larger scale. It will require a broad-based, statewide movement of leaders to prepare communities for the impending intergenerational transfer of wealth. As we move forward, our development staff must create and support a system of affiliated fund leaders who work together collaboratively within peer-learning settings. When this is accomplished, the expertise and knowledge among affiliated fund leaders will increase exponentially, which will enable them to build community-wide initiatives for retaining local wealth.

5. *Partnerships*.........Discuss partnerships with other agencies, if applicable.

In addition to our partnerships with our 202 affiliated funds in 72 counties, NCF also collaborates with Great Plains Communications, which has offered ten $50,000 challenge grants to affiliated funds in communities it serves. We also work directly with Consolidated Companies, which provides challenge grants to several of our affiliated funds, as well as scholarships to students who plan to live and work in their rural areas. NCF is the lead partner and fiscal agent for HomeTown Competitiveness (HTC), a collaborative program with the RUPRI Center for Rural Entrepreneurship and the Heartland Center for Leadership Development. HTC is an intensive community development framework being implemented in 18 Nebraska communities.

6. *Work Plan*............Include key dates and actions.

NCF has identified approximately 40 potential candidates who have the knowledge, experience and capacity to serve as peer mentors. Our program is in its very early stages of curriculum design and tools development; therefore, we will be working initially with about six to10 mentors. Over the course of the first year, we plan to expand peer mentor recruitment and training to include approximately 20 mentors. Our goal is to recruit, train, assign and evaluate 50 active peer mentors over a three-year period beginning January 2008. Candidates are selected based on several over-arching qualities and qualifications:

- Experience with local community leaders
- Advocacy of NCF; training received and trustworthiness
- Willingness to serve
- Topical experience
- Proactive rather than reactive approach

Candidates are then rated in topic areas of expertise. These topic areas are also used as indicators for measuring the performance of individual affiliated funds:

New Affiliation Setup	Endowment Building	Events/Celebrations
Board Structure	Donor Visitation	Marketing and
Operations/Treasurer	Planned Gifts	Communications
Action Planning	Financial Planners	
Challenge Grants	Strategic Grant Making	

Mentors will receive formal instruction and systemized tools that include updated operations and development manuals. If funding is available we will develop a password protected Web site for restricted communications, information and downloads.

Our plan calls for a certification process that includes in-person and remote training sessions, monthly networking meetings through teleconferences, and a special session at our annual Rural Philanthropy Conference in September 2008 focused specifically on mentor training and orientation.

As a first step during early development, mentor recruits will begin their service to NCF by participating in an "internship" type of role during our regularly scheduled training sessions offered to all of our affiliated fund leaders. Our mentors will play a primary role in peer learning and networking opportunities with other NCF affiliated fund leaders during the following NCF training opportunities planned in 2008:

Regional Meetings

Southwest	March 6	McCook	Northeast	April 1	Pender
Sandhills	March 11	Thedford	South Central	April 10	Shickley
West	March 13	Ogallala	North Central	April 15	Atkinson
Southeast	March 18	Nebraska City	Panhandle	TBD	Kimball
East	March 25	David City	Northwest	TBD	Gordon

Each of these meetings will be customized to meet specific regional needs, but generally mentors will begin their orientation by helping with instruction and discussion on endowment building, action planning, board development and transition, and strategic grant making.

Rural Philanthropy Conference
Mentors will be available for one-on-one consulting and will help facilitate break-out sessions during NCF's second national Rural Philanthropy Conference, September 10-12, 2008, in Nebraska City. Last year's conference drew 93 rural community leaders from 13 states and nearly 20 Nebraska communities. The conference focuses on the intergenerational transfer of wealth, building endowments, board development, donor visitation, strategic grant making, action planning and NCF's HomeTown Competitiveness community development framework, focusing on entrepreneurship, philanthropy, leadership and youth attraction.

Annual Training
Mentors will play a key role during our annual training for affiliated funds in November 2008 in McCook. Held in conjunction with our annual celebration, this session provides an interactive learning environment for affiliated fund leaders across the state. Topics include strategic planning, marketing, board development, youth engagement, donor cultivation and more. Participants will also explore McCook's success with its HomeTown Competitiveness efforts during a special "field day."

Remote Call-In Sessions
Mentors will contribute to periodic one-hour call-in sessions with NCF staff members and fund leaders to discuss tried and true best practices, as well as innovative and creative approaches for successful fundraising for community and organization funds.

Mentor Visitations
In addition to these scheduled public events, mentors will assist NCF staff by responding to specific individual requests from community leaders seeking basic information about establishing or growing a community foundation affiliated fund. We anticipate approximately 35 mentor visitations during our initial year of development. The following job description details expectations for the NCF Mentor position:

Key Mentor Responsibilities:
- Respond to requests for information and questions about local fundraising
- Share knowledge through NCF training manuals, information packets, organizational tools
- Communicate by telephone, letter, e-mail and on-site meetings as necessary
- Share personal experiences with community foundation work
- Share community success stories and examples
- Communicate value of being an NCF affiliate
- Refer complex questions and issues to NCF staff
- Communicate activities and outcomes with NCF staff

Skills required:
- Personal expertise working with community volunteers and donors
- Ability as a storyteller to share NCF success stories and vision
- Motivational communicator to get commitment and action
- Team player
- Self-starter/self-motivated
- Task oriented
- Relationship builder

Compensation:
- Reimbursement of out-of-pocket expenses, including mileage, meals, phone calls, lodging and supplies
- Honorarium to the Mentor's local community foundation endowment fund

7. *Evaluation Plan*…...State how proposed objective(s), activities and outcome(s) will be evaluated.

Mentors will be required to submit written reports on their activities and services with affiliated funds to which they may be assigned on a short-term or long-term basis. NCF staff will evaluate mentors' performance based on both qualitative and quantitative data we gather from tracking the activities and progress of the affiliated funds they work with.

NCF has developed an analysis of each of its community-based affiliated funds' strengths and weaknesses based on 15 key indicators. We have also assigned an "activity level" rating of A) High Performing, B) Aspiring, and C) Status Quo to each fund. Below is a draft of indicators for levels of activity necessary for positive affiliated fund outcomes:

	(A) High Performing	(B) Aspiring	(C) Status Quo
Board Meetings	Monthly meetings	Quarterly or annually	Seldom meet
Board Engagement	Take initiative / Active	Polite listeners	Not active
View of Future	Positive / Abundance	Concerned	Scarcity / Worried
Purpose / Mission	Change the future	Unclear	Focused on projects
View of Assets	Build and grow assets	Maintain assets	Preserve limited asset
Board Contributions	100% have given	Approach others first	Waiting for outsiders
Planning Process	Goals / Timelines	Reactive planning	No action plan
View of Endowments	Primary focus to grow	Not growing / Wishing	No endowment
Donor Visitations	Multiple follow-ups	Sporadic	Afraid to ask in person
Challenge Grants	Seeking / Pursuing	Wishing / Waiting	Not interested
Grantmaking	Strategic / Purposeful	Minimal impact	Disburse equally to all
Planned Gifts	Actively soliciting	Hoping to receive	Waiting for windfall
Repeat Donors	Many giving annually	Most give only once	Same big donor
New Donors	Growing each year	A few new donors	Seldom a new donor
View of NCF Fees	Good investment	Concerned with costs	Trying to avoid

We also have developed an analysis of the current status of our community-based funds regarding key action areas. **Below is an excerpted selection from an analysis of funds located in one of 10 statewide regions.** NCF will use this type of evaluation tool to match mentors' strengths and expertise with affiliated fund leaders' needs.

Community-Based Funds in the Southwest Region requiring NCF and Mentors' Assistance in 2008

3=Top priority, 2=Second priority, 1=Moderate priority

Activity Level	NCF Staff	Lead	DF JJ — New Affiliation Setup	JY — Board Structure	DW — Operations/Treasurer	DF JJ — Action Plan	DF JJ — Challenge Grant	DF JJ — Endowment Building	JG — Donor Visitation	RC — Marketing/Communications	JG — Planned Gifts	JG — Financial Planners	JY — Strategic Grantmaking	DF JJ — Events/Celebrations	Last Contact
A	Eustis	DF				3		2		1					
B	Arthur	JJ				1			3		2				
C	Hayes County	JJ		1			3	2							
A	McCook	JJ				3			1				2		
B	Arthur	JJ				1			3		2				
C	Curtis	JJ		1				2	3						

To match mentors' expertise with funds that will benefit from peer learning, NCF developed a similar rating system for its potential mentors. **Below is a skills analysis of potential mentors located in the Southwest, one of 10 statewide regions.** The table indicates that there is significant experience with launching challenge grants and building endowments. There is less expertise in new affiliation setup and working with financial planners. Therefore, these are areas that may require staff assistance when responding to requests for assistance.

Potential Mentors in Southwest Region requiring training and support in 2008

3 = High level of experience   2 = Moderate level of experience   1 = Limited level of experience

Mentor Candidates		New Affiliation Setup	Board Structure	Operations/Treasurer	Action Plan	Challenge Grant	Endowment Building	Donor Visitation	Marketing/Commun.	Planned Gifts	Financial Planners	Strategic Grantmaking	Events/Celebrations
Dan R.	Imperial	1	2	3		2	3	1				1	1
Elna J.	Imperial		1		1	3	3	3	3			1	2
Kathy T.	Maywod	1	3			3	2					2	
Mark G.	McCook	2	3	3	2	1	2	1		2	2	3	2
Don H.	McCook		3	1		3	2	3	1		2	3	2
Pete P.	Ogallala	2	3	3	3	3	3	3		2		3	3
Jack P.	Ogallala	2	3	1	1	3	3	3	3	2			2

These tracking tools, along with regular reports from our mentors and fund leaders, will be used to measure monthly progress toward the goals of increasing sophistication and success for both our mentors and the communities they are assisting.

8.   Leadership…………..**List those who will direct and evaluate the project and their qualifications.**

Doug Friedli, NCF Development Director, and Jana Jensen, Assistant Development Director, will be directly responsible for program implementation. Jeff Yost, NCF President and CEO, will oversee program design, evaluation and quality control of the peer mentoring program.

Doug joined NCF in 2002 and is responsible for developing new and existing affiliated funds, working with more than 1,000 fund advisory committee members. A lifelong Nebraskan, Doug enjoys living in Nebraska City and working in small towns with volunteers and nonprofit organizations in rural Nebraska. He has served as a volunteer board member for the Lyons Community Foundation, the Nebraska City Community Foundation, and the Lewis and Clark Visitor Center Foundation. He has served as a director of the Nebraska United Methodist Foundation and the Southeast Community College Foundation. Prior to joining NCF, Doug was a community banker for 34 years.

Jana Jensen works from her home office near Bingham, Nebraska, providing technical assistance to the NCF affiliated funds in primarily the western portion of the state. She also works with the HomeTown Competitiveness program as a site leader in the Sandhills/Mullen area and in Perkins and Chase counties. Prior to joining NCF in 2002, Jana was Vice President of Member Services for the Nebraska Cattlemen organization. She currently serves as the Fundraising Coordinator for the Nebraska Cattlemen Research and Education Foundation.

Jeff Yost joined NCF in 1998 and became President and CEO in 2003. Under his leadership NCF has sustained 20 percent or more annual growth rates for each of the past five years. Jeff serves as co-founder and chair of the HomeTown Competitiveness collaborative, an award-winning community economic development partnership. He is the immediate past chair of the Council on Foundations CEO network, a board member of the Nebraska Microenterprise Partnership Fund, and an adjunct faculty member for the University of Nebraska's Department of Public Administration.

B. FINANCIAL PLAN
1. *Project Budget........*List expenses, sources & amounts of income, including this request, and their status (confirmed, pending, anticipated, not yet applied for).

Please see attached budget sheet at the end of this proposal for a detailed explanation of revenues and expenses for a three-year program. All grant requests are pending at the time of this proposal submittal.

2. *Positive or Negative Balance...................*Discuss any balances in the project budget and your plans for raising funds or using a surplus.

The first year budget shows a positive balance of $10,750. Each of the three foundations listed (W.K. Kellogg Foundation, Peter Kiewit Foundation and the Cooper Foundation) has invited NCF to submit proposals requesting support for this community development training and assistance program; however, NCF has not yet received commitments for any specific level of support.

3. *Development Plan...*Outline your plan for funding this proposal now and in the future.

Program start-up during the first year of a three-year development plan will require significant investment in NCF staff time and mentor tools and technologies. We are developing a plan to secure ongoing funding for our peer mentoring program through a number of sources. The Ford Foundation and the W.K. Kellogg Foundation have each challenged NCF to build a multi-million dollar endowment to support our work in the future. Earnings from this endowment will provide partial funding. Thus far, NCF has raised $3.8 million in contributions and expectancies toward its $6.0 million goal.

4. *Timing.....................*State when funding would be needed.

Funding is requested on or before June 30, 2008.

C. BACKGROUND OF THE ORGANIZATION
1. *History & Mission...*A brief description.

The Nebraska Community Foundation exists to help concerned individuals mobilize charitable giving in support of the betterment of Nebraska communities and organizations. The Nebraska Community Foundation, a 501(c)(3), was established in 1993 to serve communities, organizations and donors throughout Nebraska. The Foundation provides a range of services including financial management, strategic development and education/training.

In the past six years, the Nebraska Community Foundation has grown by more than 27 percent annually, expanding to more than $66 million in assets and expectancies. Over the past five fiscal years, 29,608 contributions were made to one of the Foundation's 202 affiliated funds. Charitable giving is enabling communities to create a powerful tool for community and economic development. Today, over 2,000 local leaders serve as advisors to our affiliated funds, helping to shape their community's future. Since inception, the Nebraska Community Foundation and its funds have reinvested over $65 million in Nebraska and its hometowns.

2. *Programs.................Key programs not otherwise included in this application*

The Nebraska Community Foundation is increasingly recognized nationally as a model for rural philanthropy. The Ford Foundation and the W.K. Kellogg Foundation continue to make major investments in NCF for further development of its unique, community-based system, and for sharing the NCF model with community foundations across the nation. NCF's approach to grassroots mobilization has been broadly disseminated through activities with the Council of Foundations and through media outlets such as the *New York Times, The Wall Street Journal* and *Successful Farming Magazine.*

In addition to traditional fund management and investment services, NCF takes a proactive approach to increase rural community vitality through intentional development of broad-based community philanthropy. NCF helps local leaders recognize local assets, including human, social, cultural and entrepreneurial assets. It encourages leaders to build on these assets by investing charitable dollars in people and programs for economic growth.

NCF uses the impending transfer of intergenerational wealth as a call to action for its affiliated funds statewide and for philanthropic leaders on the national level.

In 2001 NCF completed analyses of both the magnitude and the peak of the transfer of wealth for Nebraska and each of its 93 counties. Based on those findings, NCF estimates that $94 billion will be transferred in the next 50 years in rural Nebraska (750,000 citizens). More important is the timing, with 86 of 93 counties experiencing their peak transfer on or before 2039; 26 very rural counties will peak on or before 2014. By comparison, the peak transfer for the United States as a whole will not occur until some time after 2050, if ever, as each year the country continues to become larger and wealthier. In rural Nebraska, commonly referred to as land-rich and cash-poor, engaging the middle class in estate planning to ensure that they include gifts to sustain their communities is essential to capitalize on this opportunity.

Using the transfer of wealth opportunity to devise an asset-based community development strategy, NCF has created the HomeTown Competitiveness (HTC) collaborative. HTC helps communities identify reachable goals and strategies focused on four pillars of reversing rural decline: building leadership and community capacity, engaging young people, fostering local philanthropy and endowment building, and supporting entrepreneurship. HTC helps community leaders with endowment building by giving prospective donors a better case statement. In 2005, HTC was awarded one of only six $2 million grants (from more than 180 applications) from the W. K. Kellogg Foundation to build a statewide Entrepreneurship Development System. Today HTC is being implemented in 18 Nebraska communities and is replicated in 13 other states.

The Grant Award Letter

Eleanor Cicerchi

Jubilant as we all are when the grant award letter or package arrives (even if we have already heard informally that the grant has been made), "receiving the grant is not the end but a beginning," observes Jan Newcomb, former president of the Charleston Symphony and former grantmaker, now a consultant. "The award letter is your work plan," she continues. "Consider it a contract."

As the development officer, or staff member with development responsibilities, you are a key liaison between the foundation and the people who will be managing and reporting on the use and impact of the funds. Thus you are also key to fulfilling that contract. How well you do that—especially if this is a first-time grant from a foundation or if a grant modification is needed at some point—can be a deciding factor in whether the grant is renewed and the relationship between your agency and this foundation flourishes— indeed, how well your entire grantsmanship program flourishes.

This chapter is organized into three sections: first, a checklist to use in determining what the award letter and/or grant agreement requires your organization to do in return for accepting the funds; second, a description of common elements of grant award letters and grant agreements; and third, a deeper discussion about what the award letter says about modifications to the grant, consequences of noncompliance, and support for terrorist activities. These three aspects of award letters are discussed in greater depth because of their importance.

The 5-point checklist

Foundation officials and senior development professionals I interviewed for this chapter have coalesced around five "must dos" when you receive the grant award letter in order to be sure that your organization is in compliance with the contract.

1. First, it is essential to read the grant award letter and the grant agreement, if there is one, very carefully. Note the steps your organization must take to be in compliance with the contract, and record the due dates for interim and final reports. Also identify the people you will need to work with in order to gather and report on grant outcomes. Remember, the foundation is not expected to remind you about the requirements of the grant beyond the award letter and probably won't. That is the responsibility of the development officer or, in small organizations, the CEO.

2. Check to see if there is a signature page or a grant agreement that must be reviewed and signed by an officer of your organization. You won't receive the check or wire transfer until the requested documents, with the required signature(s), have been received by the foundation. Check, too, to see if the foundation requires additional information such as a more recent audit than the one you sent with the original proposal.

3. Share the award letter and grant agreement with the project director—or the staff member(s) or team responsible for the work funded by the grant—immediately. The project director needs to be aware of how the money is to be used, the outcomes data to be collected, and the types of interim or final reports that are required.

4. Also share the award letter and grant agreement with your finance office as soon as it is received, but not just to be sure that the grant is coded and logged into your financial management system. You need to share with the finance office what the letter says about how the funds can and cannot be used and whether or not the foundation requires that the money be kept in a segregated fund. Paying attention to how the funds are to be used is especially important if the grant is for project support, if it is a challenge grant, or if you plan to use a portion for indirect costs, such as administrative support and facilities management. Hopefully, you have negotiated indirect costs and other details with the grantor during the grantseeking process, but if you haven't, this is the time to settle such questions. "No surprises" is guidance equally appreciated by the grantor, the project director, and your finance office. Also, if you receive the grant near the end of the year, and if it is to be used to support projects in the next fiscal year, or if you receive a multi-year commitment, be sure you make your finance office aware of that. You are at least partially responsible for ensuring that the money is available during the fiscal year in which it is to be spent.

5. Alert your program and finance managers to the *due dates* for interim and final reports. It is likely that the foundation will expect both a narrative report and a financial report. Most development officers don't have direct access to the data they need to write such reports or the authority to obtain it, so they need to establish a process to obtain that information on a timely basis. This was often a challenge in international agencies in which I have worked. The narrative and financial data may need to come from a country office half a world away. Program staff may be in the field or on vacation, and you may not be fully aware of their schedules. Allow for long lead times to avoid a last-minute rush or having to ask the foundation for an extension.

Marie Orsini Rosen, vice president for development at Millennium Promise Alliance and former senior director, resource development at Save the Children, shares the reporting cycle for the grant with both program and finance staff as soon as the award letter is received. She also notes key dates and "tickler" dates in her online calendar, as well as in the development database, three months before a report deadline, with reminders at two months and one month in advance. Her calendar reminders are all color-coded—as are the hard-copy files—to indicate the type of funder and type of grant.

Terry Billie, assistant vice president for institutional advancement at the New York Hall of Science, also uses color-coding for her online calendar, designating specific times during the day for meetings, phone calls, and writing. "My calendar for today is a veritable rainbow," she noted in an interview. "Often you have brilliant people on staff, brilliant in the sense of big ideas, but they may not be as skilled at tracking details. That's where the development office comes in. You simply must have controls in place if you are going to meet the requirements of the grant."

Types and contents of award letters

Some award notifications are simple letters congratulating the agency on receiving the grant. They often request a formal acknowledgement letter as a well as a narrative report on grant outcomes and a fiscal accounting of project expenses and income at the end of the grant period. (Even if these are not specifically requested, consider them standard practice and a minimal requirement.)

A grant award letter from The Eugene and Agnes E. Meyer Foundation, of Washington, D.C., for example, states succinctly, "The grant has been made on the basis of your recent proposal. Your acceptance of the enclosed check signifies your agreement that grant funds will be spent only for the activities described in that proposal." The outline of the final report, with the organization name, grant amount, grant purpose, grant number, and report due date, is attached. It specifies the information to be included in the narrative report: the goals and outcomes of the grant, the process used to achieve them, and the evaluation criteria that had been identified in the proposal; evaluation results; target population involvement, and sustainability, on the next phase of this effort; the additional resources obtained; and how those resources will be used to sustain the program. The financial statements required include, in this case, a financial statement for the organization for the current fiscal year and a financial statement for the grant, showing budgeted versus actual revenue and expenses for the term of the grant. Such letters may be used for general operating support funds or for special project grants.

Here is a concise four page document including a grant award letter, reporting requirements, and grant agreement form from the Bush Foundation of St. Paul, Minnesota.

Bush Foundation

332	Suite	St. Paul,	Tel: 651-227-0891
Minnesota	East 900	Minnesota	Fax:651-297-6485
Street		55101	

July 13, 2007

Ms. Sara L. Engelhardt, President
Foundation Center
79 Fifth Avenue
New York, NY 10003-3076

Dear Sara:

I am pleased to tell you that at its recent meeting, the Board of Directors of the Bush Foundation adopted a resolution providing for payment to Foundation Center the total sum of $180,000 to support the work of the Center during 2007-2009.

The period for which these funds are granted extends from July 12, 2007 to July 31, 2010. Payment(s) will be made by the date(s) listed in the following table provided you meet the terms of the Agreement:

Schedule Date	Amount
August 31, 2007	$60,000
August 31, 2008	$60,000
August 31, 2009	$60,000

This grant and notice of approval are subject to your meeting the terms and conditions as outlined in the attached "GRANT AGREEMENT." Grant funds may be spent only for the purposes granted. Uncommitted funds at the end of the grant period must be returned to the Foundation unless other arrangements have been proposed beforehand.

The Bush Foundation places information about grants we make on our website. This includes a link to your website (if applicable). Please let us know in writing at the time of your acceptance of this grant if you would prefer that your website not be listed.

The Bush Foundation will expect to receive from you an acknowledgment of your acceptance of this grant and of the conditions prior to disbursement of funds.

We wish you well with your program.

Sincerely.

Anita M. Pampusch
President

AMP/JA/lk#24564
Enc.   ACCOUNTING DEPT.

JUL 2 0 2007

Handwritten annotations:
$60,000 2007 — Independent Fdn. Unrestricted New Pledge
$60,000 2008 — Independent Fdn. Unrestricted New Pledge
$60,000 2009 — Independent Fdn. Unrestricted New Pledge

BUSH FOUNDATION
GRANT AGREEMENT*

As a condition of a total grant of $180,000 from the Bush Foundation to Foundation Center to support the work of the Center during 2007-2009, the undersigned hereby agrees:

1. To use the funds only for the designated purpose and not to use the funds for any purpose prohibited by law, including those purposes specified in Section 4945 of the Internal Revenue Code (see box below).

2. To repay any portion of the grant which is not used for the designated purpose.

3. To submit progress reports of activities carried on under the grant, evaluations of what the grant accomplished, and complete financial reports detailing use of the grant funds according to the attached schedule.

4. To maintain records of receipts and expenditures and to make its books available to the Bush Foundation at reasonable times.

5. That this is not a pledge, grantee will not incur any liabilities in reliance on the grant until the funds are received, and any grant payment may be discontinued, modified, or withheld at any time when, in the judgment of the Bush Foundation, such action is necessary to comply with the requirements of law or this agreement.

6. Consistent with Executive Order 13244 and the Patriot Act, no portion of the grant will be used to support terrorism, or will be diverted to other individuals or organizations which have assisted, sponsored, or provided financial, material, or technological support for terrorists or persons associated with terrorists.

FOUNDATION CENTER

By _____

Title *Executive Vice President*

Date *7/23/07*

#24564

> IRS Code Section 4945 describes "lobbying" as a variety of activities including attempting to influence either elections or legislation at any level of government. Influencing legislation is further described as attempts to influence public opinion on a legislative subject or direct communications with those who formulate legislation. An exception is made for nonpartisan analysis, study, and research.

*Please contact the Bush Foundation before or after the agreement is signed with any questions you may have about the period covered by the grant, the schedule of grant payments, the schedule of reports required, or the desired format for project and financial reports. Adjustments to grant periods and uses of Bush Foundation funds are possible but may require approval by the Bush Foundation Board of Directors. **One signed copy of this Grant Agreement must be returned to the Bush Foundation before payment can be made. The second copy is for your files.***

BUSH FOUNDATION REPORTING REQUIREMENTS*

FOUNDATION CENTER

Schedule Date	Type of Report	Grant #	Project	Project Start Date	Project End Date	Grant Amount
July 31, 2008	Interim Project Report	24564	to support the work of the Center during 2007-2009	7/12/2007	7/31/2010	$180,000
July 31, 2008	Interim Financial Report	24564	to support the work of the Center during 2007-2009	7/12/2007	7/31/2010	$180,000
July 31, 2009	Interim Project Report	24564	to support the work of the Center during 2007-2009	7/12/2007	7/31/2010	$180,000
July 31, 2009	Interim Financial Report	24564	to support the work of the Center during 2007-2009	7/12/2007	7/31/2010	$180,000
September 30, 2010	Final Project Report	24564	to support the work of the Center during 2007-2009	7/12/2007	7/31/2010	$180,000
September 30, 2010	Final Financial Report	24564	to support the work of the Center during 2007-2009	7/12/2007	7/31/2010	$180,000

* A suggested format based on the Minnesota Common Report Form can be downloaded at www.bushfoundation.org (click on "Grants to Organizations" and "Report Form").

BUSH FOUNDATION
GRANT AGREEMENT*

As a condition of a total grant of $180,000 from the Bush Foundation to Foundation Center to support the work of the Center during 2007-2009, the undersigned hereby agrees:

1. To use the funds only for the designated purpose and not to use the funds for any purpose prohibited by law, including those purposes specified in Section 4945 of the Internal Revenue Code (see box below).

2. To repay any portion of the grant which is not used for the designated purpose.

3. To submit progress reports of activities carried on under the grant, evaluations of what the grant accomplished, and complete financial reports detailing use of the grant funds according to the attached schedule.

4. To maintain records of receipts and expenditures and to make its books available to the Bush Foundation at reasonable times.

5. That this is not a pledge, grantee will not incur any liabilities in reliance on the grant until the funds are received, and any grant payment may be discontinued, modified, or withheld at any time when, in the judgment of the Bush Foundation, such action is necessary to comply with the requirements of law or this agreement.

6. Consistent with Executive Order 13244 and the Patriot Act, no portion of the grant will be used to support terrorism, or will be diverted to other individuals or organizations which have assisted, sponsored, or provided financial, material, or technological support for terrorists or persons associated with terrorists.

FOUNDATION CENTER

By _____

Title ___President_____

Date ___July 27, 2007_____

#24564

> IRS Code Section 4945 describes "lobbying" as a variety of activities including attempting to influence either elections or legislation at any level of government. Influencing legislation is further described as attempts to influence public opinion on a legislative subject or direct communications with those who formulate legislation. An exception is made for nonpartisan analysis, study, and research.

*Please contact the Bush Foundation before or after the agreement is signed with any questions you may have about the period covered by the grant, the schedule of grant payments, the schedule of reports required, or the desired format for project and financial reports. Adjustments to grant periods and uses of Bush Foundation funds are possible but may require approval by the Bush Foundation Board of Directors. *One signed copy of this Grant Agreement must be returned to the Bush Foundation before payment can be made. The second copy is for your files.*

Other grant agreements are packages that may contain an acknowledgement form to be signed by your CEO and/or a several-page grant agreement. These multi-part grant agreements specify the grant period, describe the purposes for which grant funds are to be expended or refer to the original proposal, and specify detailed terms and conditions of the grant. Such conditions may include:

- **Use of funds.** All grant agreements commit the grantee agency to use the funds in accordance with the proposal or as set forth in the grant agreement. Typical language may read, "Grant funds may be spent only for the purposes granted. Uncommitted funds at the end of the grant period must be returned to the foundation unless other arrangements have been proposed beforehand." A grant agreement from the Charles Stewart Mott Foundation for general operating support states, "This letter contains the entire agreement between your organization and the Charles Stewart Mott Foundation, and there are no conditions or stipulations, oral or written, governing the use of the grant funds other than those contained in this letter." The named project in the letter is "General Purposes."

Here is an example of one grant agreement letter from the Charles Stewart Mott Foundation of Flint, Michigan, for a general purpose project (other agreements may differ).

CHARLES STEWART
MOTT FOUNDATION

February 29, 2008

Ms. Sara L. Engelhardt, President
Foundation Center
79 Fifth Avenue
New York, NY 10003-3034

Project: General Purposes
(Grant No. 2000-00539.03)

Dear Ms. Engelhardt:

We are pleased to inform you that the Charles Stewart Mott Foundation has approved a grant in the amount of $120,000 to the Foundation Center for the above-referenced project for the period January 1, 2008 through December 31, 2009.

Grant Payments

This grant will be paid as follows:

$60,000 upon receipt of your acceptance
$60,000 on March 1, 2009

Payments are conditioned upon the Mott Foundation's receipt and approval of all reports due prior to the payment date. (See the "Reports" section of this letter.)

The Mott Foundation reserves the right to discontinue, modify, or withhold any payments that might otherwise be due under this grant, to require a refund of any unexpended grant funds, or both, if, in the Mott Foundation's judgment, any of the following occur:

1. Grant funds have been used for purposes other than those contemplated by this commitment letter.

2. Such action is necessary to comply with the requirements of any law or regulation affecting either your organization's or the Mott Foundation's responsibilities under the grant.

Ms. Sara L. Engelhardt
February 29, 2008
Page 2 (#2000-00539.03)

3. Your organization's performance under the grant has not been satisfactory. The Mott Foundation in its sole and absolute discretion will determine whether performance has been satisfactory.

The Mott Foundation's judgment on these matters will be final and binding.

Mott Foundation Contact Person

Please direct all correspondence (including all required reports) and questions relating to this grant to Nick Deychakiwsky, Program Officer.

For answers to general questions about the Foundation's grant procedures, we encourage you to visit our online grantee resource at www.mott.org/toolbox/resources.aspx.

Use of Grant

Under United States law, Mott Foundation grant funds may be expended only for charitable, scientific, literary, religious, or educational purposes, as specified in section 170(c)(2)(B) of the Internal Revenue Code. This grant is to be expended solely in support of the objectives detailed in your proposal submitted January 18, 2008.

Your organization shall not, directly or indirectly, engage in, support or promote violence or terrorist activities.

Your organization confirms that this project is under its complete control. Your organization further confirms that it has and will exercise control over the process of selecting any consultant, that the decision made or that will be made on any such selection is completely independent of the Mott Foundation, and further, that there does not exist an agreement, written or oral, under which the Mott Foundation has caused or may cause the selection of a consultant.

Mott Foundation grant funds may not be used for lobbying expenditures.

Mott Foundation grant funds may not be used for re-granting to secondary organizations.

Grant Accounting

Your organization is required to maintain financial records for expenditures and receipts relating to this grant, retaining these records and other supporting documentation for five years after the grant's termination date.

Your organization is also required to permit the Mott Foundation to have reasonable access to your files, records, and personnel during the term of this grant and for five years thereafter for the purpose of making financial audits, verifications, or program evaluations.

Ms. Sara L. Engelhardt
February 29, 2008
Page 3 (#2000-00539.03)

Reports

The Mott Foundation requires the following reports be submitted for this grant:

> **For the period ending December 31, 2008, a report is due February 1, 2009.**
> **For the period ending December 31, 2009, a report is due February 1, 2010.**

The reports must include the following parts, which <u>must</u> be submitted together:

1. A **narrative report** summarizing your organization's major activities during the reporting period.

2. Your organization's **financial statements** that include the reporting period.

Compliance with Laws

Your organization may not use any portion of the grant funds to undertake any activity for any purpose other than one specified in section 170(c)(2)(B) of the Internal Revenue Code. Further, the Mott Foundation reserves the right to discontinue, modify, or withhold any payments that might otherwise be due under this grant or to require a refund of any unexpended grant funds if, in the Mott Foundation's judgment, such action is necessary to comply with the requirements of any law or regulation.

Public Information

The Mott Foundation will include information on this grant in its periodic public reports. The Mott Foundation also welcomes grantees to make announcements of grants upon return of this signed commitment letter. A copy of any release should be sent to the Mott Foundation's Communications Department prior to its dissemination. The department is available to provide assistance in your communications efforts.

Acceptance

This letter contains the entire agreement between your organization and the Charles Stewart Mott Foundation, and there are no conditions or stipulations, oral or written, governing the use of the grant funds other than those contained in this letter.

It is understood that by countersigning this letter, your organization confirms that there has been no change in its qualification as an organization exempt from income taxation pursuant to section 501(c)(3) of the Internal Revenue Code or its classification under section 509(a)(1), 509(a)(2), or as a Type I, Type II, or functionally integrated Type III supporting organization under section 509(a)(3) of the Internal Revenue Code. If any change occurs, you must notify the Mott Foundation.

Ms. Sara L. Engelhardt
February 29, 2008
Page 4 (#2000-00539.03)

If your organization agrees to the grant conditions as stated, please return, in the enclosed envelope, one complete copy of this letter with the **original signature** of an appropriate representative of your organization in the space provided. In countersigning this letter, this individual represents to the Mott Foundation that he/she has the authority to sign this letter on the organization's behalf.

This grant may be withdrawn if the Mott Foundation has not received your acceptance within one month from the date of this letter.

On behalf of the Mott Foundation, I would like to extend our best wishes for the success of this endeavor.

Sincerely,

Phillip H. Peters
Vice President-Administration and Secretary/Treasurer

PHP:jap

Our organization acknowledges that appropriate personnel have read and understand this letter, that its terms and conditions are acceptable to us, and that we will comply with those terms and conditions.

Name of Grantee ___The Foundation Center_____

Printed Name of Authorized Signer ___Sara Engelhardt,_____

Authorized Signature _____
          (This must be an __original__ signature of an authorized representative of the organization.)

Title ____President_____

Date Signed ___March 13, 2008_____

Some grant agreements include the original budget and require the grantee to guarantee that the grant funds will be spent in accordance with that budget. If the grant is for general operating support, the grantee may be required to guarantee that the funds will be spent in accordance with the charitable mission of the agency.

- **Reporting cycle.** Most grant agreements specify deadlines for providing narrative and fiscal reports: final reports at the end of the grant period and sometimes interim reports as well. Some foundations require that these reports be signed by an officer of the grantee organization.

Here is the grant award notification from the George Gund Foundation of Cleveland, Ohio, with grant reporting form and worksheet to record all budgeted expenses under the grant.

1155.

216 241 3114   1845 GUILDHALL BUILDING

Fax 216 241 6560   45 PROSPECT AVENUE WEST

CLEVELAND, OHIO 44115

The George Gund Foundation

Ms. Cynthia Glunt Bailie, Director   September 18, 2008
The Foundation Center
1422 Euclid Avenue, Suite 1600
Cleveland, OH 44115-2001

Dear Ms. Glunt Bailie:

I am pleased to inform you that the Trustees of The George Gund Foundation have approved a grant of $30,000 to The Foundation Center (Grant Number 08-218) for operating support. This action has been taken in response to your letter and proposal of July 2, 2008, and is made on the terms described below.

It is our understanding that grant funds will be used to support administrative and programming expenses of the Foundation Center Library in Cleveland.

Under the laws of our Federal Government relating to the Foundation, all grants must be used solely for educational, scientific, or charitable purposes. The objective of this grant, as indicated above and described in the background material you have provided, may be modified only with the Foundation's approval.

Grant payment cannot be made until the countersigned copy of this letter is received. In order to receive grant payment on the dates indicated below, the Foundation must receive the grant reports on the dates scheduled. For your convenience, we have enclosed a copy of our Grant Reporting Form; copies can also be downloaded from our website at www.gundfoundation.org. Please note that the completed Grant Reporting Form should be mailed to the Foundation by surface mail.

The Grant Reporting Form and any additional correspondence should be sent to Deena M. Epstein, Senior Program Officer, and should reference the 08-218 grant number. When there are press releases, photographs, and any published material about this grant and the work it has made possible, we would appreciate receiving copies.

It is our understanding that The Foundation Center has been determined to be a tax exempt agency described in Section 501(c)(3) of the Internal Revenue Code and is classified as other than a private foundation under Section 509(a) of the Code. If there is any change in this status and/or classification, please let us know promptly. In event of loss of tax exempt status under Federal laws, or a change in classification, no further expenditures of grant funds are to be made and any unspent grant funds are to be returned to the Foundation.

ACCOUNTING DEPT.

G.P-   SEP 26 2008

↑$5,000

2008
Independent Fdn.
Restricted - CL
New Pledge
TWP

The George Gund Foundation
Grant Reporting Form

INSTRUCTIONS:

These guidelines have been implemented to aid you in reporting the progress of your grant. Reports assist the Foundation in tracking the progress of programs and projects and in maintaining the required fiscal and programmatic oversight of grants. Reports are also intended to provide the grantee an opportunity to reflect on program activities and plans.

Please return a completed Grant Reporting Form by each date indicated on the Report and Payment Schedule. Reports <u>must</u> be received prior to release of grant payment. If a section or question is not applicable to your grant, please indicate so. In addition, feel free to add any supplemental information or materials that may be helpful to our understanding of your progress.

It is acceptable to retype this form on your own word processor or typewriter if you wish to do so. Although, remember to follow the same chronology and format.

Grant Number: _08-218_

Name of Organization: The Foundation Center _____

Address: _____

_____

Telephone Number: _____ **Person Completing Form:** _____

E-Mail Address: _____

Foundation Contact: _____ **Amount of Grant:** _____

Purpose of Grant: _____

Type of Report: Semi-Annual _____ Annual _____ Final _____

NOTE:

1. **Scheduled reports <u>must</u> be received prior to release of payment. Please consult your grant letter for report due dates. Submission of reports on or before due dates will ensure payments on schedule.**

2. **Do not include final or interim reports with any requests for future support. The two must be submitted separately.**

I. **General Program Information** (Please make additional copies if needed.)

I-A. **OBJECTIVES**

OBJECTIVE	ACTIVITIES
Please list the original objectives of your proposal in this column:	What activities has your organization conducted during this reporting period to meet each objective? List below:

I-B. **FACTORS IMPEDING OR CONTRIBUTING TO SUCCESS OF THE GRANT**

What internal and external factors have contributed to or impeded the success of this grant? Discuss below (add on separate sheets of paper if necessary).

I-C. **EXPERIENCES AND ADVICE**

Based on your experience thus far, what would you have done differently if you had the chance? What would you do the same? What advice would you give to another organization planning to conduct a similar program project? (Add on separate sheets of paper if necessary).

II. Budget

Provide a detailed list of all expenses incurred during the duration of this project which have been paid for with The George Gund Foundation grant. **NOTE: This should <u>not</u> include your organizational budget.**

ITEM	BUDGETED	ACTUAL
	$	$
	$	$
	$	$
	$	$
	$	$
	$	$
	$	$
	$	$
	$	$
	$	$
	$	$
	$	$
	$	$
	$	$
	$	$
	$	$
	$	$
TOTAL	$	$
UNEXPENDED BALANCE		$

- **Records and audits.** Some foundations require the grantee to retain original substantiating documents for grant expenditures and that these records be made available for review by the foundation, if requested. A grant agreement may also ask the grantee to agree to an on-site visit or audit during or after the period of the grant.

- **Prohibition of use of grant funds for propaganda activities or influencing legislation or a public election.** This includes carrying on voter registration drives, inducing or encouraging violations of law or public policy, or causing any private inurement or improper private benefit to occur. The grantee's signature on a grant agreement with this language ensures that the foundation is not knowingly in violation of the Tax Reform Act of 1969 (TRA 69), which, among other things, limited the amount of lobbying any nonprofit can do. Dr. James A. Smith, historian, former foundation officer, and now vice president and director of research and education at the Rockefeller Archive Center, explains that TRA 69 created a new regulatory regime for foundations. It was the culmination of nearly twenty years of increasing Congressional scrutiny of private foundations and their operations. With regard to lobbying, TRA 69 places more restrictions on foundations than on public charities, and that has not changed in the intervening 40 years. Hence many foundations use grant agreements that spell out the prescriptive language in TRA 69 with regard to lobbying and disqualified persons.

- **Multi-year grants.** When making multi-year grants, most foundations recognize that expenditures may differ slightly from the budget presented in the original proposal. The W.K. Kellogg Foundation, of Battle Creek, Michigan, for example, states in its award letter: "Based upon receipt and approval of your annual progress reports, future payments will be made as scheduled; over/under expended funds from the prior year will not cause a change to the originally committed payment schedule." However, a report is required at the end of every year, if not more often. Some foundations make second and third payments conditional: they are made only if a satisfactory grant report is received. If so, this will be spelled out in the award letter or grant agreement and, of course, has accounting ramifications.

- **Notice of management and organizational changes.** Some grant agreements require that the grantee notify the foundation of changes within the organization, such as the resignation of the CEO or program director, which could impact the agency's ability to carry out the grant. Although this is not usually a requirement of the grant, it is good stewardship to notify grantors of such changes within your organization as soon as the information is public, rather than waiting until the end of the grant period or until word reaches the foundation through other channels.

- **Intellectual property.** In line with growing interest in protecting intellectual property rights, foundations increasingly include in grant agreements language about ownership and re-publication of materials produced with grant support. Most acknowledge that publications, reports, conference proceedings, and other materials produced with grant funds are the property of the grantee, but specify that the foundation has rights to receive copies, even to publish the material in its own publications. A recent grant agreement sent by a corporate foundation to the Foundation Center reads, "All intellectual rights, products and materials under this grant, while they might be the property of the grantee, [the foundation] has the right to receive copies under this grant." The grant agreement form used by California Endowment, of Los Angeles, California, links its right to publish material produced with an Endowment grant to its commitment to make the results of its funding available to the public: "Any information contained in publications, studies, or research funded by this grant shall be made available to the public following such reasonable requirements as The Endowment may establish from time to time. Grantee grants to The Endowment an irrevocable, nonexclusive license to publish any publications, studies, or research funded by this grant at its sole discretion."

- A grant agreement sent out by the John S. and James L. Knight Foundation—perhaps understandably, given the foundation's roots in publishing—is far more detailed:

  > Grantee and the Foundation agree that all copyright and other interests in materials produced as a result of this grant shall be owned by the Grantee organization. To ensure the widest possible distribution of such materials and ensure that they enter and remain in the public domain, the Grantee organization and any individuals who may have some interest hereby grant to the Foundation a non-exclusive, transferable, perpetual, irrevocable, royalty-free, paid-up, worldwide license to use or publish the materials or other work products arising out of or resulting from Grantee's use of the grant funds and any earnings thereon, including all intellectual property rights, and to sublicense to third parties the rights described here. Grantee, at Foundation's request, agrees to execute any additional documents required to effect such license.

- **Verification of the grantee's legal status.** Many grant agreements also require verification of the grantee's legal status and require notification if that status changes, even if a change of status is merely proposed. The California Endowment uses this wording:

  > This grant is specifically conditioned upon Grantee's status as an eligible grantee of The Endowment in according with this section. Grantee warrants and represents that it is one of the following: (a) a tax-exempt organization under Section 501(c)(3) of the Internal Revenue Code of 1986, as amended (the "Code"), and is not a private foundation[1] as defined in Section 509(a) of the code, (b) a governmental

---

[1] The prohibition of grants to private foundations—they most likely would be private operating foundations—is not a universal prohibition among foundations. Because of the additional accounting requirements for foundation grants to private foundations, small and mid-sized foundations, which have smaller staffs or none at all, may be unwilling to take on the additional responsibility. If you work for an operating foundation, as I have, it is important to notify prospective grantors, especially small and mid-sized foundations and donor-advised funds, of your agency's legal status early in the grantseeking process.

unit referred to in Section 170(c)(1) of the code, or (c) a college or university that is an agency or instrumentality of a government or political subdivision of a government, or owned or operated by the same, within the meaning of Section 511(a)(2)(B) of the Code......Regardless of Grantee's current tax status, Grantee will notify The Endowment immediately of any actual or proposed change in tax status.

- **Acknowledgement of the grantor.** Another typical section of a grant agreement requires the grantee to acknowledge the foundation in printed materials relating to work supported by the grant. Some require approval of press releases and other printed references to the foundation in advance of publication. The California Endowment's grant agreement reads, "Grantee shall ensure that The Endowment is clearly identified as a funder or supporter of Grantee in all published material as a funder or supporter in its annual report (if any). All proposed Grantee external communications regarding The Endowment shall be submitted first to The Endowment for its review and approval."

Some foundations actually have explicit instructions about content and procedures to follow, and this information is included with the grant award notification. Here are the publicity guidelines of the Koret Foundation of San Francisco, California.

Publicity Guidelines

In making this award, Koret is supporting the work that you do. We ask that you support *our* work in turn by acknowledging and including Koret in your publicity efforts. We would like to work with you to communicate our shared goals to the public and to other organizations. Please follow these guidelines:

- Please acknowledge Koret Foundation support in all announcements, media interviews, publications, web postings and advertisements related to the program.

- Please send us a copy of any press release regarding this award for review *before* it is distributed. We would like to be informed of any media coverage and to be sent copies of articles, photos, web stories, etc.

- Please send copies of marketing materials, ads, newsletters, website postings or articles that mention the program and Koret's support of it for review by Koret's Communications Officer *before* they are printed.

- The following language should be used to identify the Koret in press releases and other publications. Consult with your program officer before making any changes:

  An entrepreneurial spirit guides Koret in addressing societal challenges and strengthening Bay Area life. Investing in strategic, local solutions, we help to inspire a multiplier effect – encouraging collaborative funding and developing model initiatives.

  In the San Francisco Bay Area, Koret adds to the region's vitality by promoting educational opportunity, contributing to a diverse cultural landscape, and bolstering organizations that are innovative in their approaches to meeting community needs.

  With our roots in the Jewish community, we embrace the community of Israel, especially through Koret Israel Economic Development Funds (KIEDF); we believe that economic stability and free market expansion offer the best hope for a prosperous future.

  At Koret, we understand our responsibility to make an impact – to honor the legacy of our founders, and to find long-lasting solutions that improve people's lives.

We would appreciate it if you would inform us of any special events, photo opportunities, openings or other presentations related to the award as far in advance as possible.

We strongly encourage you to use Koret's logo in your printed materials. It is available upon request. Please contact your program officer.

If you would like to discuss publicity matters with Koret, please ask your program officer to put you in touch with our communications officer.

Thank you, and we wish you every success with your work.

Modifications/extensions of grants

Some grant agreements require the grantee to notify and seek approval from the foundation for any "material" changes to the budget. This is such an important aspect of the grant award letter and grant management process that it is dealt with below in greater detail.

A grant proposal represents a plan, and there are certainly times when things don't turn out as the grantee had hoped, for any one of many reasons. Foundations recognize this, too, and often include in their grant award letters or grant agreements wording about the types of change that they want to be made aware of. Jan Newcomb states, "You need to know what constitutes a change big enough to warrant a phone call or a letter to the program officer." This is not usually a major concern with general operating support grants, since the grant has been made for the operations of the entire agency, but it can be very important with project funding, a grant that requires matching or supplementary funding, and/or multi-year grants. A recent grant agreement from the Walter & Elise Haas Fund specifies, "Any significant changes in the purposes for which grant funds are spent must be approved in writing by the Fund before the funds are spent. Prior permission from the Fund is required for budget revisions of 10% or more for line items over $1,000."

An award letter from the W.K. Kellogg Foundation states:

> "The following types of revisions must be requested separately and be approved by your foundation program officer prior to completing the financial reporting form:
>
> - Budget revisions that significantly change the current reporting period
>
> - Budget revisions requiring changes to the total foundation commitment amount and/or changes to the start or end dates of the grant as these constitute a revision to the original commitment agreement."

Consequences of noncompliance

Many foundations are flexible about extending the grant period or accepting changes to the budget. But there are often provisions in grant agreements that require that unexpended funds, or funds spent for activities that were not included in the original proposal or grant agreement, be returned to the foundation. Additionally, a foundation may state explicitly that the agreement with the grantee includes the right to make a site visit or review financial reports pertaining to the grant. The grant agreement from the Charles Stewart Mott Foundation, for example, states that records and supporting documentation relating to a grant must be kept by the grantee for five years after the grant's termination date. Further, "Your organization is also required to permit the Mott Foundation to have reasonable access to your files, records, and personnel during the term of this grant and for five years thereafter for the purpose of making financial audits, verifications, or program evaluations."

"These kinds of provisions protect the foundation in the event that the project never goes forward or there are substantive changes to the project, or even misdirection of grant funds," explains Suzanne H. Lee, president and CEO of the First Community Foundation of Pennsylvania.

"This is one reason why you need to have a grant management system," notes Terry Billie. If, for example, there are no records about how the grant needs to be used or the types of reports that need to be filed, all or a portion of the grant may have to be returned to the foundation. Jan Newcomb recalls how she avoided what could have been a serious problem with a major regional grantmaker. New to her position, she "…looked for but couldn't find a single piece of paper that described the purpose of a particular grant or the expectations of what we would deliver," she recalls. "So I called the foundation. They were delighted that I called and very willing to send a replacement grant agreement."

This story underscores the importance of making the award letter and grant agreement available to those who need to know about them (like your own financial staff) and making these documents the starting point of the grant management process. Dwight Burlingame, assistant director of the Center on Philanthropy at Indiana University, explains that he is unaware of a foundation going so far as to take legal action to recover unexpended or misused funds, but he knows of many examples of pressure foundations can apply when requesting a financial review and the potential return of the funds. "Often there is an audit to determine how much money has been spent on which activities. On the basis of the results of the audit, the unexpended or misapplied funds are returned."

Janne Gallagher, vice president and general counsel of the Council on Foundations, explains the legal force of a grant. "A grant is not a contract, but it is a legally binding agreement. A private foundation is empowered to investigate the reported misuse of funds." She adds, "There is a 'presumption of sorts' that funds not expended or expended for activities outside the scope of the proposal and grant agreement are to be returned to the foundation. There are no reported court decisions about such cases," she states, "but the court-appeal databases include only decisions at the appellate level. Lawsuits may have been initiated and settled at lower levels."

Negotiations with program officers about modifications and extensions of a grant are dealt with elsewhere in this guide. For now, suffice it to say that even in the absence of court decisions that substantiate the legal force of a grant agreement, the degree to which the grantee complies with the grant agreement has a significant impact on the establishment of trust between grantor and grantee and certainly the possibility of future grants.

Anti-terrorism requirements

The Patriot Act that followed the events of 9/11 has had broad reach, even extending to grantmaking and the agreements that formalize a grant. Because of concerns that gifts to nonprofits that work internationally or with non-Western populations could end up in the hands of terrorists, the Patriot Act prohibits public charities from knowingly supporting terrorist groups and foundations from making grants to charities that do. This is the reason behind stipulations found in grant agreements today prohibiting the grantee from using grant funds for acts of terrorism or to support persons or organizations that have been identified as terrorist groups (USA Patriot Act of 2001 and U.S. Executive Order 13224, Executive Order Blocking Property and Prohibiting Transactions With Persons Who Commit, Threaten to Commit, or Support Terrorism). The Rockefeller Foundation includes in its grant agreements a simple clause referring to the prohibitions: "Anti-Terrorism. You hereby confirm that [agency] complies with all U.S. anti-terrorism laws and regulations, including Executive Order 13224 and the Global Terrorism Sanctions Regulations set forth in 31 CFR Part 594." Kristin Curry, director of foundation, corporate, and government relations at the Newark Museum, notes that increasingly she has noticed examples of foundations' requiring charities to indicate that they do not support terrorists earlier on as part of the grant application, rather than in the grant agreement. Either way, it is a factor in working with foundations, and it needs to be taken seriously.

For many U.S. nonprofits, this is not a concern. However, Marie Osini Rosen, of Millennium Promise Alliance and formerly of Save the Children, has observed unintended consequences of this provision in the Patriot Act. "Many aid agencies by mission are nonpolitical and nonpartisan," she notes, "and they do their best to comply with Patriot Act requirements. Finding the language and logic to paint a realistic picture of what it is like to deliver aid in developing countries and especially countries in crisis can be both difficult and frustrating," she continues. "It is often the distinction between principle and pragmatics. For example, things can get challenging when delivering services to children whose adult family members may for some reason require scrutiny. Per their missions, most agencies will not willingly refuse to extend services to their beneficiaries, especially children. Yet the Patriot Act provisions can interfere with the agencies' missions. In these cases, the Patriot Act can cast a long shadow."

Conclusion

In the end, the grant award letter or grant agreement, as any contract or memorandum of understanding must do, makes explicit the expectations of the grantor to ensure that funds intended for the benefit of the public good are, indeed, used as such. It also spells out the guarantees the grantor makes to the grantee. To the degree that the grant agreement is proscriptive, it reflects the policies and procedures of a carefully regulated segment of the philanthropic community. None of that takes away from the fact that, in making the award to your organization, the grantor is recognizing the value and capabilities of your organization and entrusting to you the funds and the opportunity to further your mission. In requesting reports, the foundation is also interested in helping your organization assess and reflect on how well you achieved your objectives, what challenges you faced, and what you have learned. It is not unusual for a grant award letter to end with words similar to these from the Robert Wood Johnson Foundation: "We are privileged to welcome you again to the Foundation's community of grantees," or from the Eugene and Agnes Meyer Foundation: "We wish you continued success and look forward to hearing more about your work in the year ahead."

3

Managing the Grant Project

Debbie Rosenberg Bush and Diane Carillo

Introduction

This chapter is written from the point of view of the nonprofit grantee. In the text that follows, when we refer to "you," that's who we mean. The advice we provide here is applicable whether you are a development officer for a large or medium-size nonprofit, a program director who has been tasked to run a foundation-funded project, the executive director of a small nonprofit, or even someone wearing many hats running a one-person shop, perhaps as a volunteer. What matters is this: you've just received a grant and you need to know what to do next. As a grant recipient, when you accept a check for a grant, you are essentially also accepting and agreeing to a variety of responsibilities. Receiving a grant is a good thing—but managing a grant costs your organization time and money. Therefore, when you accept a grant, all systems need to be streamlined and efficient.

These systems will help you and your organization to maintain successful and growing relationships with your funders by demonstrating that you are a good steward of their grant funds—i.e., you are using the grant funds for the purpose for which they were given. These systems will help you inform the funder when circumstances require that your organization make a change from the original plan. They will also help make your life easier. They will save you time and will help you become a more successful fundraiser.

As two long-time grantees who have worked in foundation fundraising at several major nonprofits, as well as smaller organizations, we have identified all of the elements that we consider when we receive a grant. This chapter offers a series of detailed checklists on everything you need to know to successfully manage a grant project. Managing a grant inevitably includes a lot of "stuff" and many details to keep track of. You and the donor will generate a lot of paper and a lot of information, and it is your job to manage hard-copy and electronic documents and files. It is also important that you utilize your donor database to best effect in managing the grant and the grantee/grantmaker relationship. Your role also includes ensuring that good communication is a key element of that relationship. Many of the points that we make are discussed in greater detail in other chapters in this book.

Receiving the grant

If you are reading this chapter, you have applied for and been notified that you have received a grant for your organization. Congratulations! This is indeed reason to take a moment to celebrate the fact that your organization has demonstrated to a funder that its work is important and worth supporting. It also means that you have done a good job in presenting the case for your organization and the particular project for which you have requested support. It means that you have fulfilled the proposal application requirements and presented a work plan to be followed in carrying out the project. From here on, much of your work will involve keeping all parties informed and on track.

Here are some things you might do right away:

- Jump up and down (do the happy dance), and pick up the phone and call the donor to say a big "thank you."

- Share the good news with your own program and financial staff and all appropriate management (including board members who may have assisted with the application). Celebrate with your co-workers and other interested parties.

- Write a prompt, thoughtful, and specific letter formally acknowledging receipt of the grant and what it is for. It is best to send this letter within a week of receiving the grant.

Defining roles: Wearing many hats

Depending on the size and complexity of your organization, the responsibilities for managing the grant project may be meted out among several people or even several departments; or they may fall entirely on your shoulders. The chart "Cast of Characters" describes what the various functions are and indicates who within your organization might be charged with carrying them out. Throughout this chapter, we will refer to the charted functions and responsibilities; you should bear in mind that the individual filling these roles might be one of your colleagues or it might be you.

Cast of Characters

Role	Responsibilities	Performed by, in Organizations of Different Sizes		
		Small	**Medium**	**Large**
Point of Entry	*This is the person in your organization who receives and opens the mail.* Receive and open mail; look for correspondence with funders, including grant award letters and checks. Distribute the paperwork for processing.	You or one of your co-workers	Receptionist Development Office Manager or Assistant	President's office Program or Department Head Vice President of Development Development Officer
Grant Solicitor *(In some organizations, the Grant Solicitor and the Grant Manager—below—are the same person. If you are reading this chapter it is probably you.)*	*This is the primary person who was involved in soliciting the grant.*	You or any of your co-workers or board members	Development staff Program staff Executive Director President Volunteer	Development staff Program staff Executive Director President Volunteer
Grant Manager	*This is the person who has the primary responsibility for everything related to managing this grant.* The Grant Manager communicates and coordinates with all of the other roles and is the liaison with the funder. Functionally, this is the link between the funder and all other organizational staff. A key aspect of this is processing the grant paperwork.	You or any of your co-workers with development responsibilities	You or any of your co-workers in the Development Department	You or any of your co-workers in the Development Department
The roles below are part of grant management overall and may be performed by the Grant Manager or the other individuals noted:				
Data Entry	Enter data in manual and/or automated systems: -Calendars -Donor database -Proposal tracking -Financial records	You or any of your co-workers	Data entry staff	Data entry staff
Finance	Business systems, including: -Accounting -Bookkeeping -Finance -Official recordkeeping for auditors, etc. -Budgeting: i.e., appropriately showing the grant in the organization's budget, including recording the funds for restricted or unrestricted use.	Bookkeeper Accountant Executive Assistant You	Finance and Budget staff Accounting staff or outside accounting firm	Chief Financial Officer Budget Office Accounting Office Chief Investment Officer
Program Staff	Implement the grant, including spending the money according to the plan, budget, and timeline in the original proposal.	You or one of your co-workers	Program Director or staff members	Vice President, Program Director, or other program staff members
Public Relations/Communications	Prepare and produce materials in which donor recognition may be included according to donor obligations, donor preferences, and your organization's guidelines.	You or one of your co-workers	Public Relations or Communications staff member	Vice President, Communications Director, or outside agency/consultant

Grant requirements and responsibilities to the donor

After the initial celebration, it's time to get down to business. Receiving a grant entails a variety of stated and implied responsibilities. Regardless of the size of the grant or the level of detail required by the funder, the basics remain the same:

- Start with the award letter. Sometimes it is a very simple communication. Sometimes it includes details on when reports are due and may entail a very detailed grant agreement. In any case, you as the development staff person in charge of receiving this grant need to take a close look at this letter so that you can appropriately lay out what steps your organization needs to take moving forward.

  Typically, institutional funders like foundations will send official notification of a grant via hard copy—something in writing. This is the document from the donor that outlines your organization's obligations. Some funders will include an actual "grant agreement," which needs to be signed (usually by your chief executive officer or chief financial officer) and returned for both parties' signatures. This is essentially a contract between the funder and your nonprofit organization. Even in the absence of a paper "grant agreement," common practice dictates that you are indeed entering into a financial and legal partnership with the funder—and your job is to be the administrator of this relationship and also the steward of the grant funds. Keep in mind that the original proposal and proposal budget that you submitted with your request for funding are now part of the financial and legal agreement between your organization and the funder. The original proposal—including the budget, timeline, staffing, project elements, and deliverables—is part of the grant agreement, the official record of what is being funded. Essentially the awarding and acceptance of a grant is a process that is allowed under IRS rules for grantmaking by organizations that have been authorized to make and accept charitable contributions.

- The next step is to copy (photocopy/e-mail/scan) the requisite paperwork. (For the purposes of this chapter, we refer to "paperwork," but it can indeed be electronic.) Photocopy and distribute the check or other payment (e.g., stock or wire transfer), all donor communications received with the award, and a copy of the original proposal, including the original budget, along with a copy of report formats, requirements, and instructions for reporting, if available.

- This is a good time to set up a work file for yourself. A work file helps to make your life easier by providing a place for you to gather materials related to the grant as they come your way. Placing copies of all paperwork in your new work file will help save time later on when you need to monitor and report on progress on the grant. Save a copy of *everything* related to the grant in your work file, including all e-mails and notes from phone conversations and funder meetings related to the grant. Doing this at the very outset and continuing to do so over the life of the grant, rather than waiting until the end, will serve you well and save you time in the long run.

A useful analogy is what you may do to prepare for filing your income taxes. A year in advance, you may or may not set up a folder or a box for your tax receipts, forms, and everything related to filing taxes. You may or may not actually put things in the folder or box cumulatively throughout the year. You may have set it up so that the correct forms automatically get sent to you, or you may know how to find the particular forms online. You may also know or have identified someone with expertise—an accountant or someone who can do your taxes or who is familiar with your finances. Having the systems in place, knowing who can help, and having resolved potential problems (e.g., lack of documentation) in advance of your tax filing date will enable you to worry less. Just setting up the system doesn't do it, however. Actually using the system is what makes your life easier.

- In a timely fashion, process any paperwork requested by the funder in the award letter. This may include return of papers signed by a particular staff member (your CEO, CFO, other officer of your organization, or you). Copy and be sure to share signed materials with your financial staff.

- You will want to be sure that the individuals responsible in your organization for data entry and the relevant financial staff member, especially if this falls under two different departments, are receiving and keeping all appropriate records of the grant. You will also want to have mechanisms in place from the start of the grant project to ensure that program staff working on the funded project allocate and report on expenditures under the grant appropriately.

Grant entry and processing form. Basically, a grant entry and processing form is a tool to assemble essential information, and it also serves as a vehicle for informing all parties who need to know about anything related to the grant and to the specific funder. The grant entry and processing form provides all information needed by staff in charge of data entry and your finance department, and it provides a bridge between the two. (We realize that in some small organizations, especially those that are volunteer-run or one-person shops, both the data entry individual and the finance department will be you!)

Most important, this form helps to ensure that the grant funds have been correctly allocated in both your organization's donor database and its general ledger.

The grant entry and processing form helps to guarantee accountability, e.g., that all appropriate parties in your organization are informed about the proper, approved use of the funds. A copy of all paperwork associated with the grant should be attached to the grant entry and processing form and distributed to all need-to-know staff. The form should be used as a cover sheet for distributing all official paperwork related to the grant. Larger organizations may already have a grant entry and processing form. For smaller organizations it's a good idea to introduce such a tool.

Here is a sample grant entry and processing form appropriate for a foundation grant:

Foundation – Grant Processing and Entry Form

Foundation_____   Date: _____

Prepared by: _____   Solicitor:_____Database ID#_____

[ ] Unrestricted [ ] Restricted to Program _____ in _____ Department

---

Total Amount of Grant: _____   Check received? [ ] yes [ ] no

-Income Source Code: _____
-Appeal/Campaign Code: _____
-Department Receiving and Spending Funds Code: General Fund _____ or Department _____
-Project Fund Code: _____

Pledge/Pledge Payments
Total amount of the pledge: $_____
Payment amounts: $_____   **Payment Year:** _____
     $_____   **Payment Year:** _____
     $_____   **Payment Year:** _____

Gift Notes for Database: include Grant Period
_____
_____
_____
_____
_____
_____
_____

Acknowledgement plan: 1. _____
     2. _____
     3. _____

[ ]Report(s) & Proposal Renewal Plan in database   [ ] Calendar updates

Hard copies to: [ ] **Gift Processing/Finance (official record)**   [ ] Foundation File   [ ] Work File
Scanned copies to: [ ]Program Staff   [ ] Donor Recognition staff
     [ ] _____   [ ] _____   [ ] _____

Remarks/Donor Obligations (Reports, etc.)/Calendar/Schedule:
_____
_____
_____
_____

Attachments: [ ] Grant Letter/paperwork
     [ ] Copy of Proposal (including narrative, timeline, budget, etc.)

7/20/09 Debbie Rosenberg Bush and Diane Carillo/Chapter 3, "Managing the Grant"

Coding the grant

With help from your financial and data entry colleagues you will want to identify and create codes specific to your organization so that the grant money can be allocated and expended appropriately. Examples of codes you might need include:

- **Income source:** Foundation, Corporate Foundation, Family Foundation, Government Grant, Individual Donor

- **Appeal/campaign code:** Annual Fund, Capital Campaign, Special Project, Program Proposal

- **Department receiving and spending funds:** General Fund, Education Department, Other Named Department

- **Project fund code:** Annual Conference, Lecture Series, Youth Interns, etc.

Restricted vs. Unrestricted Funds

All grant funds received by your organization are either unrestricted or restricted. It is vitally important to distinguish between restricted (e.g., available only for application to specific salaries or other expenses as identified in the original proposal budget) and unrestricted grants (e.g., available for general operations or any other aspect of the organization), and to remind others in your organization about which grants are restricted and which are not.

- The grant entry and processing form should state whether the grant is unrestricted or restricted and, if restricted, for which specific program or purpose.

- Grant funds that are restricted to support a specific program cannot be used for general operating support. Similarly, grant funds that are restricted for one specific purpose cannot be used to support another program.

- Your job is to ensure that the grant funds are expended according to the purpose for which they were given.

Recognizing the donor

Gifts and grants are often recognized in an organization's newsletter, brochure, program materials, web site, and the like. Such recognition is often specified as a requirement in the grant award letter. Some funders require recognition; some funders want their support to remain anonymous. Obviously you will want to follow the funder's wishes.

And you will need to work with staff within your organization to make sure that the funder is recognized appropriately. You are also the liaison with the donor to secure approval of the recognition language, if necessary.

Some organizations have threshold levels for recognizing gifts and policies in place for recognizing grants at different levels in different formats. It is important that you be consistent when adhering to funder requirements while following your own organizational guidelines. Keep in mind also that donor recognition will be a key element of your organization's annual report.

Here are some recognition guidelines:

- Identify and communicate donor recognition details and requirements to all need-to-know staff.

- Review all printed and online materials to ensure that the donor recognition is correct. See additional information below under "Announcing the grant."

- Corporate funders typically have very specific requirements for recognizing their contributions, which are often referred to as "sponsorships." You may want to run your recognition language, and exactly where it will be listed, past your corporate donor's public relations department. If you do this, be sure to allow extra time, since the corporation may require several layers of approval.

- Of course, no donor recognition should be made public until official notification of the grant has been received by your organization in writing.

Scheduling the deliverables and next steps

Receipt of the grant is also the time for you to schedule those steps that are triggered by such receipt. While it may seem too soon, you should already be thinking about interim and final reports and the renewal proposal. This is the point where you will set up internal systems to ensure that all grant requirements are met on time.

Deadlines really matter when it comes to effective grant management. Funders expect you to meet their deadlines, and they expect you to notify them as early on as possible if it looks as if you won't be able to do so. If program staff members working on the funded project need more time to complete it or to fully expend the funds before the end of the grant period, call the funder to explain the situation and politely request more time. Do this well before the grant period is up and certainly well in advance of the reporting deadline. Funders are typically receptive to this type of request as long as it isn't made at the last minute. Deadlines are important to funders because they relate to their own board meeting cycles and are tied into their own financial accounting. Missing a deadline can mean that you miss an entire funding cycle, and thus you may be delayed in getting your next grant. It is also standard practice for funders not to continue to pay out pledges or to renew funding for grantees who do not meet their deadlines.

Sample Grants Management Calendar

January 2010

Sunday	Monday	Tuesday	Wednesday	Thursday	Friday	Saturday
					1 Holiday	2
3	4 ALERT Smith Foundation Proposal	5	6	7	8	9
10	11 Jones Foundation Proposal Mail Date	12	13	14	15 ALERT Brown Foundation Report	16
17	18 Doe Foundation Proposal HARD DATE	19	20	21	22	23
24	25	26	27	28	29 White Foundation Rept Mail Date Black Foundation Ppl HARD DATE	30
31						

Legend: Red=ALERT (At least three months in advance of the donor's deadline/HARD DATE, begin the work/remind all staff)
Blue=Mail Date (Plan to mail one month prior to donor's deadline/HARD DATE)
Yellow=HARD DATE (Donor's deadline)

Within your organization, you are the person responsible for making sure that deadlines are met. Missing a deadline damages your reputation with your funder and possibly in the larger foundation funding community.

Following are some suggestions about ways to ensure that you meet your deadlines and maintain a good relationship with your funder:

- Update your database and set up "alert/start-to-think-about-it" dates, mailing dates, and hard dates for reports and other deliverables; at the same time, schedule a date for grant renewal if applicable.

- Maintain a calendar of due dates. This can be done by setting up a separate grants calendar in your Outlook or other software system.

- As you are setting up your own internal systems for managing the grant, be sure that you have communicated the schedule for required reports to the relevant program staff.

- Regularly review due dates with development and program staff who will be working on the grant and the requisite report(s). This will keep the work on the grant on track, as well as giving you early warning if delays or departures from the original plan need to be communicated to the funder.

- Update your internal financial records, moving the proposal from "pending" to "funded" and record "money in" by program category or other pertinent category. (It is important to maintain your own financial records regarding results of all proposals that you have submitted. This will serve as a control document to check against your finance department's records for periodic reconciliation.)

- Set up a reporting file and accumulate articles, sample materials, photographs, anecdotes, and evaluations from program participants, and whatever other information seems relevant, so that these materials are available when it comes time to write the grant report. Be sure to include kudos about the project or program from those who have benefited from or observed it, and in particular any favorable media coverage. Develop a good working relationship with all those involved in implementing the grant and ask that, on an ongoing basis, they send you updates for the reporting file.

Announcing the grant

Sometimes a funder requires an official announcement of the grant, and sometimes it is part of your own institutional practice. In either case, such an announcement can be a very powerful tool for using the grant to leverage additional funding.

- Where appropriate, develop a press release or other written communication announcing the grant and acknowledging the funder. Be sure to keep "anonymous" funders anonymous.

- Check the donor recognition requirements for the funder's preferences and, where necessary, request the funder's permission to acknowledge the grant in written materials and online.

- Include mention of the funder's support in new proposals and communications with other funders.

- Ensure that all donor recognition promises are met. Additional information about announcing and recognizing the grant is included elsewhere in this guide.

Monitoring the grant

It's important to remember that the program staff actually does the work for which the grant funds have been obtained. Development staff members are the ones charged with keeping in touch with the program staff to make sure that the funded work is being carried out according to the terms of the grant as set forth in the proposal and the grant award letter—and that the work is proceeding on schedule. Here are some suggestions for your own due diligence:

- Regularly check in with program staff on the progress of the grant; don't make assumptions that the grant funds are being spent or are being spent appropriately.

- Make sure that the grant funds are being spent in a timely fashion and according to the proposal budget and timeline; be sure that the money is being spent only for the agreed-upon elements of the proposal.

- Wherever possible, visit and observe programs and review products of the grant. Collect materials related to the grant; ensure that donor recognition is being handled correctly at events and in print.

- Invite funders to any events/activities that are products of the grant.

- If changes need to be made as the grant progresses, determine if there is a need to advise the funder of any departure from the original proposal and/or budget. You may need to formally request permission for such changes or to carry over funds to the next fiscal year. Don't depart from the original plan and/or budget under the grant without obtaining express permission from the funder. If the funder does agree to the change but does not provide written confirmation, document the agreed-upon change and send it to the funder in writing. (See below.)

- In a timely fashion, advise the funder of changes in staffing affecting the grant, including program staff and your organization's CEO.

- Don't be afraid to call the funder. Most of the time, funders are very reasonable in agreeing to modifications to the proposed grant activities and timeline, as long as the changes are in keeping with the spirit of the grant. Don't wait until the last minute to ask, e.g., the day the report is due.

Managing departures from the grant proposal, budget, timeline, and deliverables

In managing the grant, your job is to ensure that the money that has been received for a specific grant is being spent according to the funder's expectations. Your job is also to ensure that the activities that were funded are executed and completed on time and in accordance with all of the promises made in the original proposal. This, of course, includes what was in the proposal budget. As soon as it is discovered that any element of the original proposal has changed or needs to change, it is incumbent on you to (1) advise the funder in a timely manner and (2) ask permission to proceed with the changes. Examples of items to be sure to bring to the funder's attention include:

- A change in staff leadership

- A change in partners involved in the project

- A change in the timeline

- A need to spend more money than anticipated on grant-funded activities, the inability to expend the grant funds on time, or the need to divert funds from one type of expense permissible under the grant to another

- Any significant departure from the original proposal

It is important that you work with your program staff to identify and convey project and budgetary changes in a timely and accurate fashion and to seek and receive permission from the funder—ultimately in writing—to proceed with the changes. Failure to do this will not only adversely affect your relationship with the funder, but it can also result in the funder's requesting the return of the grant funds.

Advance permission from the funder is needed to carry over funds beyond the specified grant period or to extend the grant for any reason. No presumption should be made about grant extensions. Although foundations will often grant permission to carry over funds and to extend grant periods when there is a good reason, it is better to avoid this, if possible, unless there is a very good reason. Best practice is to complete the grant project on time and expend all the funds as originally laid out in the grant proposal. Requesting a grant extension is not fun. It generally involves your having to write and submit an additional report. It also means that you may well delay your ability to apply for and receive the next grant for this or perhaps any other project. On the other hand, unanticipated things do come up, and the more complex the grant project the more likely they are to occur.

As noted above, the foundation world, particularly the group of funders in your field or region, is probably very small. Funders talk to one another. Protect your reputation and keep your funder apprised of changes in a timely fashion. Make requesting grant extensions the exception rather than your default. If it takes your organization too long to implement a project and expend the grant funds, it reflects poorly on your ability to get work done as promised. That may come into play when the funder is deciding whether to continue to invest in your organization with additional grant funding.

Sometimes receiving a grant is a call for a somewhat muted celebration, for example if the funder does not give you the full requested amount that is necessary to conduct the proposed project. In this case, your organization will probably need to secure the remaining funds from another source, which takes time and creates a good deal of uncertainty. Or you may need to provide the balance of funding needed from your organization's unrestricted operating funds, a decision that will need to be made by your financial staff and your CEO. In some very specific instances, it may even make sense for your organization to decline the grant if it is clear that you truly will be unable to perform what is expected with the resources available. Please refer to the Troubleshooting Guide in Appendix A for more information.

Evaluation

The evaluation requirements for grants vary widely, but, at a minimum, funders want to know something about the results of the project that they funded—and whether their grant funds were used effectively. While evaluation is covered more extensively elsewhere in this guide, here are some steps you should take as part of effective grant management:

- Just as soon as you receive the grant award, establish a system for tracking the items you will need to report back on to complete the evaluation plan laid out in your proposal.

- On an ongoing basis, check with program staff to be sure that evaluation elements are being collected and that final evaluation data will be available for inclusion in the grant report.

- Ask program staff routinely to collect user feedback, quotes, anecdotes, statements, etc. from participants. Quotes in particular will come in handy when it comes to illustrate the success of a program.

- Funders are increasingly looking for outcomes as distinct from activity reports, e.g., for a job-training program, how many people got jobs versus how many participated in the program. There is a growing body of literature about how to improve grant evaluations.

Preparing the report

No grant project is complete until the final narrative and expense report have been submitted and approved by the funder. The report is the primary means by which you tell the funder how your organization spent its money; whether or not your plan worked, and if not, why not; and, of course, if your organization did a good job. Keep in mind that for many funders it may be far more important that you achieved the best possible outcome using their grant funds than that you strictly adhered to every single item in your original grant proposal.

The production of the full report is very much a collaborative process. Yes, you helped secure the grant, but it is the program staff who executed the work. These staff members are in the best position to describe how the grant funds were spent. Again, grant reports are covered elsewhere in this guide. Here are some practical tips to get you started thinking about them:

- Send an e-mail alert to everyone who needs to give input for the report, outlining exactly what is needed and when it is due to you. It is important that you build in ample time for the creation and review of the financial part of the report. The report on expenditure of grant funds must clearly and correctly align with what was in the original proposal budget. Set up a schedule for working with program and financial staff in order to deliver the report on time; build in requisite time for review by all necessary staff— your CEO, vice president overseeing the program area, accounting staff, etc.

- Check to determine the funder's most recent reporting requirements and preferred reporting format. Share these instructions with the people who will be working with you on generating the report. Report guidelines vary widely in level of detail and format. Examples are included in Chapter 7 of this guide.

- Work with your program staff to collect all pertinent information in a timely fashion and to develop the written document. The final product must be concise and well written. A grant report is a writing product, so a good writer needs to be part of the process.

- You will need to decide who is the most appropriate person to actually draft the narrative and to compile the financial report. Sometimes that person will be you. If the report is likely to be technical in nature, the program staff should write the narrative report, and you should edit it. Program staff members who were responsible for spending the money are responsible for producing an account of how they spent it. Note that, in some cases, the funder may require that your chief financial officer sign off on the financial report. So that additional step must be figured into your timetable.

- Ask a good proofreader to edit the report. Always use spell check.

- Write a gracious cover letter to go along with the report. Be sure to thank the funder for the grant.

- Copy your report, cover letter, and the face copies of enclosures. Keep copies of original enclosures where possible. You never know when these might come in handy.

- Deliver your report on time.

- Verify that your report has been received.

- File a copy of the report in the donor's file.

- File a copy of the report in your own work file as one means of gearing yourself up for the next report and/or grant request.

- If a board member or other friend of your organization assisted in securing the grant, as a courtesy, you might want to send that individual a copy of the final report with a note of thanks.

More information on this topic will be found in Chapter 7.

Renewal funding

If you have shown yourself to be a good grantee, your funder may consider your organization or your project for further funding. Simultaneous with the delivery of the report, you may be allowed to deliver a renewal request for the project or for funding for another project. You'll need to verify that these can be done together. If the funder requires that a renewal request be sent separately, consider saying something in your grant report cover letter about your interest in being in touch soon regarding a request for future support.

- Some funders explicitly require that a report be submitted, reviewed, and approved *before* you can submit a renewal proposal. Additional payments on a multi-year grant may be contingent on receipt and approval of the report on the prior year's grant. A check may only be released after the report is accepted. You'll want to refer to your grant award letter for your funder's requirements.

- Be sure to thank the funder for past support.

Keeping required records

Certain documents are required to be kept on file for specified periods of time. Even if the funder does not specifically indicate what needs to be retained and for how long, at a minimum, the following must be kept in your donor file: the proposal, the grant award letter, a copy of the payment, a copy of the acknowledgement of receipt of payment, and schedules showing that funds were expended per the grant award. These records are critical to your organization's adherence to legal and fiduciary responsibilities in accepting and expending the grant funds. The records will have to be made available when official audits are being done. For that reason alone you must be sure that you have copies of them handy to provide upon request.

In addition to fulfilling the legal and fiduciary requirements for your organization, keeping these records accurately and in a readily accessible manner also benefits you directly, by enabling you to locate them at a moment's notice, should you receive a call from your auditors, from the funder, or from your own program or administrative staff. It will also save you time when you yourself have to look up information about the grant. Being able instantly to put your finger on needed documents demonstrates to any interested party who might be calling with questions about the grant that you are on top of the information, thus enhancing your professional status and reputation as an effective steward of grant funds. In addition, having a complete record of a grant allows new staff members who join your organization to gain a sense of the larger picture, and it paves the way for good grant management and continuity in the face of staff changes.

Note that a written acknowledgement of receipt (in letter or other hard-copy format) is a requirement of all foundation grants.

Organizing the official donor and grant files

Foundation fundraising typically generates a lot of paper and electronic documents and files, all of which you must maintain. Even in this time of electronic recordkeeping and the push for "paperless" offices, you are required to maintain certain documents in hard-copy format for access by funders, auditors, and the IRS. Therefore, it is important that you, in concert with your financial staff, set up and maintain for requisite periods of time all appropriate paperwork that relates to the award of every grant your organization receives. Earlier we supplied a short list of records that are absolutely required.

With increased volume of grant activity, you and your organization may need to invest in more sophisticated systems and software for recordkeeping and managing your foundation fundraising. To be competitive and to keep up with the volume of work, often an upgrade in donor management and financial software may be necessary. Acquisition of such software also requires knowledgeable staff or outside consultants to implement and then to maintain the systems. Ideally, at the most sophisticated level, your donor development system and its financial tracking component synchronizes with your organization's financial management system. In this regard, financial and development staff must work together to select, implement, and keep the system running. You may require information technology support as well.

In selecting appropriate software it is good to be cognizant of the marketplace and the most commonly used software systems. Being familiar with these systems increases your value to your current organization and will help your organization when you are in a position of recruiting knowledgeable staff.

The chart "Fundraising and Accounting Systems and Software—What Do I Need?" outlines the functions and purposes of different systems and what is needed by different organizations as they grow in size and complexity. There are many resources available to assist nonprofit organizations in selecting fundraising and accounting software packages. While the Foundation Center does not track or evaluate software packages for nonprofits, its web site provides links to others that provide this type of information. See the FAQ: "Where can I find nonprofit software reviews?" at the Foundation Center's web site.

Fundraising and Accounting Systems and Software—What do I need?

For Organizations with Different Volumes of Grant Activity

Function	Purpose	Small	Medium	Large
Calendar	Track • Deadlines • Mail Dates • Start Dates • Donor Meetings • Board meetings and other key organization dates • Special Events • Vacations	Paper calendar	Electronic calendar	Electronic calendar tied to fundraising database and software
Contact Manager	Master Address Book–names, addresses, phone numbers, e-mail addresses, web sites for funders, prospects, vendors, consultants—anyone else you are in contact with, including staff, board members, volunteers	Paper address book or Rolodex	Electronic contact list	Electronic list contained within fundraising database and software
Planner/To Do List for Action Items	Identify actions related to researching, soliciting, and securing funds and stewarding funders after receipt of a grant—such as: • Phone Calls • Meetings • Letters • E-mails • Proposals • Follow-ups • Acknowledgements • Reports • Updates • Invitations	Paper To Do list	Electronic task manager	Electronic task manager or action and activity planner tied to fundraising database and software
Proposal Tracking	Plan, implement, and follow up on Letters of Inquiry (LOIs) and full proposals that are planned for submission or have been submitted, and record their results. In conjunction with Calendar, include proposals anticipated to be sent so as not to miss new and renewal proposal opportunities. Can also be used to calculate actual and projected funds raised.	Paper list or chart	Electronic format, e.g. spreadsheets, that allows for tracking of proposals from concept to decision. Can include ability to sort information in different ways and to perform calculations.	Electronic proposal management capacity as part of fundraising database and software
Accounting	Count revenues received: pledges, cash, stock, gifts in-kind. Categorize these funds: restricted and unrestricted funds; capital; endowment. Track expenses, including appropriate coding for expenses associated with carrying out the grant for later reporting purposes, as well as obligations for sub-grants that are to be awarded from the grant funds. Fulfill legal and fiduciary responsibilities for official financial recordkeeping for your organization.	Paper tabulations and calculator	Electronic bookkeeping and accounting software	Electronic bookkeeping and accounting software tied to fundraising database and software and General Ledger. In the largest organizations where there are separate departments devoted to development and finance, systems for development and accounting recordkeeping need to be compatible and security protocols should allow for sharing of information.

Final thoughts

Although it is always exciting to hear the news that you will be receiving a grant, sometimes accepting a grant can be a bit of a mixed blessing for your organization, and it could end up costing you a lot of time and money. Due consideration should be taken regarding the value of the grant relative to the time and effort that will be required to manage it. Of course, make sure the grant that you are accepting is consistent with the mission of your organization and its capacity to carry out the work. It is possible that your organization's circumstances may have changed materially since the proposal was submitted, e.g., the lone staff member capable of doing the work has left, and it is incumbent on you to: (1) immediately discuss the situation with relevant internal staff, and (2) approach the funder about modifying the grant or simply passing on it for now.

As you've seen, being a good steward of a grant awarded to your organization is not an easy assignment. At the end of the day, however, you can be proud that you helped to secure the funds to make possible the good work that your organization accomplishes.

4

Communication with the Funder

John Hicks and Marilyn Hoyt

Congratulations. You've received your award letter from the grantmaker, and you've deposited the check. This may sound like the conclusion of your efforts—developing your concept into a grant proposal, meetings and exchanges with the potential funder, and a lot of anxious weeks (perhaps even months!) awaiting the funder's response. But, a grant marks a new phase in your relationship with the donor. Now that the foundation has chosen to make an investment in your program, you have a new partner with whom you must communicate.

Embrace the moment and the opportunity. "An educated consumer is our best customer," said Sy Syms, founder of Syms Clothing. In accordance with this adage, you will need to educate your best customer—your donor. Here are some reasons why:

- For a foundation, grant management involves a designated professional on the foundation side working with a group of colleagues and/or trustees to monitor the progress of their investment. The better educated your key contact(s), the better your chances of maintaining the investor relationship for the long term.

- While grantmakers may have experience and expertise in your area, most acknowledge the existence of highly specific nuances relative to how an individual organization works most effectively within its community or with its constituency. Educating your donor about the challenges and opportunities facing your organization and the audiences you are trying to help makes the foundation a smarter investor down the road.

- Managing expectations is a very important part of good grantsmanship—for both the donor and the recipient. Without clear, consistent, and quick communication, expectations can go awry and, not surprisingly, the relationship can suffer.

In this chapter we will explore how to communicate effectively with a grantmaker, beginning with your acknowledgement and acceptance of the gift. We'll also take a look at how to communicate with a donor outside of the regular reporting cycle to ensure that you are acting as a responsible steward of their investment, even if it means occasionally sharing disappointing news.

First things first—Say "thank you"

Acknowledging a contribution is as simple as saying "thank you," and as complex as the variety of ways that that appreciation may be communicated to various parties within a foundation. More likely than not, your grant award letter will convey congratulations on behalf of the foundation and, perhaps, its board. It will set forth expectations about uses of the approved funding. Likely, it will set forth requirements for reporting progress to the grantmaker—when and how reports are to be prepared and received. And it may outline further terms and conditions for the grant, ranging from how funds are to be managed to how the donor should be acknowledged. All of this is covered in other chapters in this guide.

The first consideration of a grantee is, "Are the terms of the award acceptable?" In the vast majority of cases, they will be. Grantmakers tend not to make things more complicated for themselves, or for you, than need be. That said, you do have the responsibility to your organization and to the funder to carefully review the expectations before you accept the grant.

Once you have determined that the grant is, indeed, acceptable, then you need to quickly affirm your acceptance to the donor. A reasonable turnaround time for a thank-you letter to the funder is 48 hours from the moment you open the envelope. If there is a reason your letter will be delayed (e.g., organizational policy that grant letters go through legal review), then notify the grantmaker by telephone that you have received the letter and set a reasonable expectation as to when the grantmaker can expect to receive your reply.

It is absolutely critical that you acknowledge the grant in writing and send this acknowledgement by U.S. mail. While an increasing number of grantmakers are embracing e-mail as a medium for communication, the art of the powerful thank-you still resides in the personal note that comes by mail. Also, remember that your letter of appreciation conveys more than thanks; with the signature of an authorized representative of your charity, you are accepting responsibility for carrying out the work you promised you would do in your grant proposal.

The close of your thank-you letter might also tell the foundation program officer that you will be happy to meet at any time to update the funder on your progress—either at your location or in the funder's offices, whichever is most convenient.

Here are examples of two short and simple thank-you letters from the Foundation Center, one to a large national donor, and the second to a regional donor.

**FOUNDATION
CENTER**

April 27, 2007

Ms. Margaret H. Einhorn
Chief Financial Officer and Treasurer
The Robert Wood Johnson Foundation
Route 1 and College Road East
P.O. Box 2316
Princeton, NJ 08543-2316

Dear Peggi: Re: Grant #053592

I am pleased to acknowledge the recent receipt of the Robert Wood Johnson Foundation's gift in the amount of $41,667. This represents the first payment on your 2007 pledge of $250,000.

Again, please accept our warmest thanks for your support of the Foundation Center.

Sincerely,

Alyson Tufts
Vice President
(212) 807-3624

Knowledge to build on.

79 Fifth Avenue • New York, NY 10003 • Tel: (212) 620-4230 • Fax: (212) 807-3677 • foundationcenter.org

New York Atlanta Cleveland San Francisco Washington DC

FOUNDATION CENTER

August 28, 2008

Dr. William T. Hiller
Executive Director
Martha Holden Jennings Foundation
The Halle Building
1228 Euclid Avenue
Suite 710
Cleveland, OH 44115

Dear Dr. Hiller: Re: Grant #C-11-08

Thank you for the Martha Holden Jennings Foundation's pledge of $5,590 for the Foundation
Center - Cleveland for 2008. During this period of significant growth made possible by the
Anniversary Campaign, we are grateful for your continued support. As requested, we have
returned the signed grant agreement, Card B, and the Certificate of Charitable Status to your
business office. Enclosed please find the signed Card A.

We look forward to keeping you informed and will report back to you on your gift. Our 2008
Annual Report will be available in mid-2009. In the meantime, please let us know if we can be of
any assistance.

Sincerely,

Alyson Tufts
Vice President
(212) 807-3624

Enclosure

Knowledge to build on.

79 Fifth Avenue • New York, NY 10003 • Tel: (212) 620-4230 • Fax: (212) 807-3677 • foundationcenter.org

New York   Atlanta   Cleveland   San Francisco   Washington DC

Having taken care of the formal appreciation for the grant, you can then move on to informal thanks. Consider sending a personal note of thanks to any foundation staff member who helped you along the way. You may find yourself dealing with foundations staffed by a small team of professionals where you have direct access to key decision makers. In short, your advocate may be the same person who signs the check. In the case of much larger foundations, you may receive a grant award letter signed by the foundation's CEO, an individual whom you have not met. Take the time to reach out and thank the staff members who have helped you in any way, most notably a program officer who has taken on the responsibility of reading your request, gathering information on your organization, and presenting your proposal to an awards committee or to the foundation's board. Your acknowledgement of his or her help and investment of time and energy is a crucial step in cementing a relationship that will benefit your organization well into the future.

Donor recognition

What about cases where your organization has promised the grantmaker recognition for its gift? Let's start with the fact that your organization should have a donor recognition policy. This policy should address the nature and degree of credit you will provide at each level of giving, and hopefully it will match what your colleagues nearby are offering by way of recognition. For instance, a $100,000 naming grant or gift for a capital campaign might provide years of recognition via a plaque at your facility and mention in your annual report, while a $100,000 grant in support of your programming might warrant mention in this year's ad campaign, newsletter, and print materials promoting the program.

Even if the grantmaker has not explicitly indicated how it wants to be acknowledged, best practice suggests that you give the funder a chance to approve the recognition you're offering before you proceed. Here are a few ways to do that:

- Include language in the thank-you note specifying the recognition you plan to offer at this grant award level and mention your willingness to discuss any changes the funders might request. For example, you might say: "It will be our pleasure to recognize your support via [list of credit opportunities you offer at this level]. Please let us know if you wish to discuss this further." Language like this allows grantmakers to respond if they wish, but does not commit you to securing formal approval for standard recognition.

- Place a phone call to vet the proposed recognition language to be included in a press release (not the wording of the entire release).

- Share proposed artwork for an acknowledgement ad with the appropriate foundation staffer.

- Ask the funder to review an interior/exterior rendering that displays the proposed placement of the funder's name on a plaque or wall.

As we've seen, acknowledging and thanking your donor is fairly simple and straightforward. That said, there are some things that you will want to avoid:

- Don't send the grantmaker a thank-you gift. Your agency is not receiving an award based on how much shared glory you provide to the donor. You are receiving a grant because you have a good idea about how to meet a real need in your community. If your thank-you gift were to be deemed of value, it could have tax ramifications for the donor. You want to make clear your intent to invest all grant money in your actual program or the operations of your organization.

- Don't route your initial note of appreciation through a colleague or board member. Focus your appreciation at the professional level first with the grantmaking representative whom you believe had the most to do with your organization getting the grant. The other personal thank-yous can be added later on.

Beyond thank-yous—Building donor enthusiasm

When you begin to engage in building relationships with your foundation donors, you need to be thinking about how they came to be your partner. And you need to think about what they are interested in, and what they need from you as a grantee in order to do their work, even to enjoy the results of this work!

Foundation giving represents a very effective way to get a lot of important work done. Each foundation chooses its own priorities in terms of the needs it seeks to address and audiences it hopes will benefit. And then, in most instances, instead of simply taking their own money, hiring staff, building buildings, and setting to work to meet those needs, they choose nonprofit partners to do the work.

In so doing, foundations greatly increase the amount of people power that can be applied to fulfill their philanthropic missions. A grant to a nonprofit may represent a relatively small percentage of total funds invested in meeting a particular need in any given year. By making grants to a number of nonprofits, the funder is able to enhance its impact dramatically. Thus, from a foundation's perspective, the work that is at the core of its priorities and values proceeds in a highly leveraged fashion when it makes a number of grants, each for a portion of the costs of an important activity, to strong nonprofits with compelling programs. If other foundations in the community are also attracted to the cause and decide to support it, so much the better.

Every grantmaker has many excellent philanthropic investment options to choose from—nonprofits that are working in an area corresponding to foundation priorities and doing very good work. Once the funder has completed its proposal review and chosen a particular group of nonprofits with which to work, that foundation has made a major commitment to meeting its own goals via the work of that nonprofit.

Let's begin with a key understanding: When a grant is made, you *already* have an important relationship with a foundation. The foundation is counting on you, according to the work described in your proposal, to meet its mission-related goals. This is not just a simple financial transaction with its obligation to expend funds per audit restrictions and then report back. This is a commitment on both the nonprofit's and the foundation's side to get solid work done to meet mutual objectives.

Viewed in this way, the plan for how to build your donor's enthusiasm and engagement becomes pretty straightforward. Your mandate is to position your foundation funder in an ongoing information stream so that the funder can follow the progress of your organization's work under the grant and personally feel some ownership of it.

Continuing to pique your funder's interest as the grant project unfolds

To help in this regard, here are some questions to ask yourself:

1. What are indicators of success in my field related to the grant I received? Typical success indicators in the course of a grant year might include the following:

- Outcomes that are special moments for people you serve: entrance into or graduation from a course of study, engagement of a particular population not previously served and visible progress as a result of that engagement, the completion and dissemination of a program model or product such as a book or report, completion of a program evaluation.

Here is an example of a cover letter that went along with a report that Georgia Appleseed sent out to stakeholders and funders about its grant-funded advocacy project:

December 29, 2008

Dear :

In your hands is the recently released statewide summary report of findings and recommendations gathered from hundreds of stakeholders sharing their 'common wisdom' about what works in Georgia's current juvenile code, what does not work, and their ideas on ways to fix the problems. The report findings solidly endorse the intent of the 2005 resolution adopted by the Georgia Senate calling for a new juvenile code in Georgia.

The release of *Common Wisdom: Making the Case for a New Georgia Juvenile Code* culminates two years of work by Georgia Appleseed on behalf of the JUSTGeorgia partnership. In the largest pro bono effort of its kind, thirteen lead law firms and 260 legal professionals conducted face-to-face interviews in each of Georgia's ten judicial districts and compiled a report for each district.

Stakeholder interviewees included judges, prosecutors, defense attorneys, parents, youth, social workers, law enforcement, victims, educators, and many more.   In addition, a public town hall meeting was held in each judicial district and ongoing input continues to be solicited through online survey tools.

The ten judicial district reports and the statewide summary report are available online at www.GaAppleseed.org/children/reports or at www.justgeorgia.org.

The findings and recommendations reported in *Common Wisdom* are intended to help inform an insightful legislative package for a new juvenile code, to be presented to the 2009 General Assembly. They also enable the voices of Georgians with the largest stakes in the system to be heard in their different contexts by public policy makers charged with the responsibility to provide justice for our children.

We hope these reports, and the common wisdom they bear, will inform deliberations at every level as Georgians, together, seek a new juvenile code and improved justice for Georgia's children and families and greater public safety for our communities.

Sincerely,

Sharon N. Hill
Georgia Appleseed

Indicators of success (continued):

- Credible recognition from outside your organization: an award for staff or program, a visit from a colleague or accrediting organization to review the funded program as an example of "best practice" in the field, a well-received conference presentation, favorable mention in an article in a professional or popular journal or blog.

- Quantitative recorded data: hours of service, number of products, number of locations, hours of operations. If your services are expanding, that's even better; but it is not necessary to grow your program in order to share good news with your foundation partner. Quality counts as much as quantity.

- Evidence that your work is becoming a model for others to emulate: Colleagues or even government agencies picking up on techniques, vocabulary, methodology, or program parameters based on the work of your organization.

2. *What have you learned that your funding representative may also want to learn as the funded activity moves forward?* The aspects of this learning that can be applied to a number of grantees and to the field at large will be of particular interest to the foundation. These may include:

- Trends in the needs of your target population that change the focus of services provided by your organization;

- Challenges in access to your service population that change the way your staff delivers the service;

- Evaluation outcomes that indicate the need for change, and how you will move forward as a result of these lessons learned.

3. *Is your nonprofit itself becoming more respected as an organization?* Indications that this might be the case include:

- An invitation to your nonprofit's leader(s) to join a prestigious panel, board, or task force; to deliver a keynote address at a conference; or to contribute to a book or article;

- Identification of your nonprofit as a model organization by a government or other accrediting agency;

- Contracts you've secured for turn-key training;

- Receipt of a prize or recognition award;

- Any kind of favorable media coverage.

4. Is your nonprofit able to truly leverage the foundation's grant in order to build your capacity to attract other funds, thereby enhancing your ability to deliver services? After the grant has been awarded, any additional resources drawn to the funded activity may be viewed as solid indications of such leverage. Sharing updates on large or unique resources directed at the foundation-funded activity is important. These may include:

- New funding of any kind, but particularly foundation grants of a significant size;

- Dedication of the proceeds from an event or annual fund to the grant-supported program;

- A special commitment of in-kind resources to the program;

- Evidence of the program's capacity to generate earned income—a success indicator in terms of its future viability and also powerful evidence of its value to those whom you serve.

Rules of thumb

Keeping it "personal" is best. A quick note, phone call, e-mail message, and/or invitation to an activity or event of particular interest leaves the foundation representative feeling reassured about the grantee/grantmaker relationship. These forms of one-on-one outreach indicate to your funder that he or she is a valued colleague who shares mutual goals, not "just an ATM," as one program officer famously noted.

When inviting a particular individual at a foundation as part of a larger group, it should be clear why that individual was included. Here are some possibilities: It may be that the invitation is for an exclusive event with a high-level guest list. Or it may be that the invitation is for a larger event focused on the area of the foundation's particular interest. Or the event is considered to be prestigious, and anyone would be delighted to be asked. Or, simply put, the event sounds like fun, and the foundation program officer might like to come with family or friends, or to offer this invitation to another staff member or intern as a treat.

Here is an example of an invitation to attend a prestigious-sounding event sent by Georgia Appleseed, to its funder, the Community Foundation for Greater Atlanta:

THE ART OF JUSTICE

MAY 20, 2008

GEORGIA
Appleseed

Sowing the Seeds of Justice throughout Georgia

Mission of Georgia Appleseed: To listen to the unheard voices of the poor, the children, the marginalized; to uncover and end the injustices that we would not endure ourselves; to win the battles for our constituency in the courts of public opinion or in the halls of justice that no one else is willing or able to fight.

Georgia Appleseed Center for Law and Justice is an independent affiliate of the national Appleseed network of nonpartisan, nonprofit, public interest law centers. Georgia Appleseed leverages the pro bono work of lawyers and other professionals to produce systemic solutions to difficult social justice problems.

Georgia Appleseed Board of Directors

A. Stephens Clay, Esq.
Board Chair
Kilpatrick Stockton LLP (Atlanta)

Dr. Portia H. Shields
Board Vice-Chair
President Emerita, Albany State University (Hampton)

Elizabeth Vranicar Tanis, Esq.
Board Secretary
Sutherland Asbill & Brennan LLP (Atlanta)

Jason Carter, Esq.
Young Professionals Council President
Bondurant, Mixson & Elmore, LLP (Atlanta)

Virgil L. Adams, Esq.
Adams, Jordan & Treadwell (Macon)

Kathy Ashe
Georgia House of Representatives (Atlanta)

The Honorable Roy E. Barnes, Esq.
former Governor, State of Georgia;
Barnes Law Group LLC (Marietta)

James H. Blanchard, Esq.
Retired Chairman & CEO,
Synovus (Columbus)

Charles C. Clay, Esq.
Brock, Clay and Calhoun, P.C. (Marietta)

Bertis Downs, Esq.
R.E.M. (Athens)

The Honorable Norman S. Fletcher
former Chief Justice, Georgia Supreme Court (ret.), Brinson, Askew, Berry, Seigler, Richardson & Davis LLP (Rome)

Jorge Forment
President & CEO,
United Americas Bank (Atlanta)

Sharon N. Hill, Esq.
Executive Director,
Georgia Appleseed (Atlanta)

G. Edison Holland, Jr., Esq.
General Counsel,
Southern Company (Atlanta)

Shell H. Knox
(Augusta)

L. Joseph Loveland, Esq.
King & Spalding LLP (Atlanta)

Catherine Z. Manning
PricewaterhouseCoopers LLP (Atlanta)

The Honorable Herbert E. Phipps
Court of Appeals of Georgia (Albany)

DeAlvah H. Simms, Esq.
(Macon)

Richard H. Sinkfield, Esq.
Rogers & Hardin LLP (Atlanta)

Terry Walsh, Esq.
Alston & Bird LLP (Atlanta)

Robert W. Webb, Jr., Esq.
Troutman Sanders LLP (Atlanta)

Georgia Appleseed
1100 Peachtree Street, Suite 2800
Atlanta, Georgia 30309
404.685.6750
www.GaAppleseed.org

Sharon N. Hill, Esq., Executive Director

Georgia Appleseed
invites you and a guest to enjoy

THE ART OF JUSTICE

THE SECOND IN A SERIES OF FINE ART EXHIBITS
SUPPORTING THE WORK OF GEORGIA APPLESEED

Hosted by Troutman Sanders LLP

Learn about Georgia Appleseed and the largest pro bono effort on
behalf of juvenile justice and child welfare in Georgia

Tour Troutman Sanders' outstanding art collection

•••

Bid on select donated works at the silent auction

•••

Enjoy cocktails and an artful buffet

Tuesday, May 20, 2008
6:00 P.M. to 8:30 P.M.

Troutman Sanders LLP
Bank of America Plaza
600 Peachtree Road, 52nd Floor
Atlanta, Georgia 30308

Business Attire • Validated parking

Please respond by May 14th to RSVP@GaAppleseed.org

Space is limited

For further information, call Theresa Brower at 404-815-6266

THE ART OF JUSTICE
CO-CHAIRS

Robert W. Webb, Jr.
Chairman & Managing Partner
Troutman Sanders LLP

Governor Carl E. Sanders
Troutman Sanders LLP

Wayne R. Vason
Partner
Troutman Sanders LLP

A. Stephens Clay
Kilpatrick Stockton LLP
Georgia Appleseed Board Chair

HOST COMMITTEE

Governor Roy E. Barnes
Barnes Law Group LLC

Charles C. Clay*
Brock, Clay and Calhoun, P.C.

The Honorable Norman S. Fletcher*
former Chief Justice, Georgia Supreme Court;
Brinson, Askew, Berry, Seigler, Richardson & Davis LLP

G. Edison Holland, Jr.
Southern Company

L. Joseph Loveland
King & Spalding LLP

Catherine Z. Manning*
PricewaterhouseCoopers LLP

The Honorable Herbert E. Phipps
Court of Appeals of Georgia

Dr. Portia H. Shields*
President Emerita
Albany State University

Elizabeth Vranicar Tanis
Sutherland Asbill & Brennan LLP

Terry Walsh
Alston & Bird LLP

Georgia Appleseed JUSTGeorgia Steering Committee Member

It is important to always look out for the foundation's interests. Items or services of material value they receive from you as their grantee must be reported. You need to be sure to communicate clearly prior to such a circumstance, so that the foundation representative can choose to opt in or out when it comes to receipt of a service or item that could raise questions for the auditor.

Communication: Less is more—for all of us!

Every one of us goes home each night knowing that e-mail messages, LinkedIn updates, Facebook friend requests, Tweets from those we are following, etc., are piling up waiting for our attention. And that's not to mention the various blogs we know we should be reading on a daily basis to keep up with the field. We can't seem to figure out the best way to segment our time so that we can manage this overabundant communication efficiently. And we feel really frustrated when we open a message that turns out to be of no particular interest or importance. Even worse is the occasional friend or colleague who fails to install antivirus software so that his or her messages infect our system. We begin to take mental note of colleagues who send us broadcast drivel, and we tend put their communiques at the bottom of the heap.

Foundation representatives are in the same boat, and their boat may be full to overflowing. Given the amount of messages they are likely to receive in various formats, the task of ferreting out those they must read, from those they probably should read, from those they can choose to ignore, is nothing short of monumental. So, your challenge as a grantee when communicating with your funder is to provide vital information in the simplest, most direct manner possible. Be sure to indicate on the subject line or the very first sentence or paragraph what the message is all about. Your program officer might not read further than that, otherwise. At the same time, all of this communication falls under the rubric of donor cultivation, and that's very important when it comes to maximizing your relationship with your funder. Since it's clear that we need to find better ways to communicate, what are the most effective choices?

What are the vehicles you can use to communicate effectively with funders?

1. Personal call

Nothing beats a personal call for impact. But, as a grantee, when you call too often, it makes you appear needy and may ultimately result in your foundation representative's "screening" your calls. The best advice is to keep phone calls to your funder few and far between and to reserve them for truly important communications that your funding representative will perceive as such. These might include the types of favorable news mentioned earlier, such as media attention, other funding received, awards, recognition, or a prominent addition to your staff or board.

If there is "bad" news of real substance regarding the funded activity or about your organization or its leadership, it is vital that you call your foundation contact immediately to inform him or her about the problem, how it came about, and what you and your organization's leadership plan to do about it. If appropriate, you might seek counsel from the funder in terms of a possible resolution to the problem. This needs to happen before the foundation representative hears this news from someone else. And be forewarned: this type of news tends to travel fast.

2. Notes and letters

Personal notes are excellent vehicles for telling and inviting. They can also be used to provide additional or follow-up details after a phone call has taken place. You should consider sending a note or letter under the following circumstances:

- After the receipt of a grant award letter or notification phone call;

- After the receipt of the grant check;

- As a cover letter attached to each proposal and report;

- As a personal invitation to join an intimate event;

- As a personal note attached to a printed invitation for a larger, more formal event, if possible indicating why the foundation program officer would care to attend (see above for a list of reasons);

- An informal note that really serves as a mid-term update on progress on the grant.

Here is a brief personal note from the executive director of Georgia Appleseed to her funding representative at the Community Foundation for Greater Atlanta; it packs a lot of information into a single page:

October 12, 2007

Ms. Lesley Grady
VP Community Partnerships
Community Foundation for Greater Atlanta
50 Hurt Plaza, Suite 400
Atlanta, GA 30303

Lesley,

I wanted to pass along this information to you in order to keep you updated on the work Georgia Appleseed is doing regarding the Juvenile Code Re-write project (now known as JUSTGeorgia).

With financial support from the Community Foundation, we were able to hire Leslie Gresham as the JUSTGeorgia project manager for Georgia Appleseed. Since coming on board in July, Leslie has been responsible for coordinating the pro bono services of over 250 attorneys who have volunteered to conduct stakeholder interviews around the State. To date, the pro bono time dedicated by the volunteer attorneys to the project well exceeds $1,000,000. In addition, Leslie is also responsible for organizing the 10 town hall meetings currently taken place around the State.

Information gained through the interviews and town hall meetings will be the basis for a state-wide report on the status of juvenile justice and deprivation in Georgia under our current juvenile code. Findings of the report will be used to inform the drafting of a legislative package for a revised Juvenile Code.

We are pleased to share this exciting update with you, and are grateful for the support from TCF that has helped allow us this strong start to the JUSTGeorgia project. Our Executive Director Sharon Hill, Leslie Gresham and I are available, by phone or to meet in person, if you have any questions.

Theresa Brower

3. E-communication

We've alluded to this issue above; it's critical, no matter what the size of your organization, that you send clean communications. You don't want to inconvenience foundations by unleashing viruses into their systems. Second—keep it short! These days the odds are good that the foundation program officer receiving your communication is opening your message on a PDA. Given that reality, a few succinct lines is much more effective than a page of text, accompanied by one or more attachments.

What is the protocol for electronic contact between grantee and funder? The fact is that best practices in this area are still evolving. But here are some interim guidelines:

- It is appropriate for a grantee to connect with a foundation program officer via e-mail, Facebook, LinkedIn, Twitter, or any other means of e-communication if (and it's a big "if") the foundation representative either uses it first to contact you or instructs you to do so.

- It is appropriate to contact a foundation program officer via an e-mail address listed on the foundation's web site, annual report, or funding guidelines. However, if your name or e-mail address is not already familiar to the program officer, the chances of receiving a reply may be slim.

- It is generally considered inappropriate to contact a foundation program officer using an e-mail address obtained via a web search or from a colleague who happens to have it. On the other hand, if a foundation officer has a Facebook or similar open-to-all web site, it is probably okay to communicate with the individual that way. However, once again, the chances of a reply are not good.

E-mail continues to be the quickest, most immediate tool for communicating with funders. It uses everyone's time most efficiently. While, depending upon the circumstances, it may be appropriate to send the same e-mail to a dozen funders or more, each message should at least appear to be sent one at a time. Otherwise the message looks like junk mail. And if there is a personal line or phrase you can add to each message, then that would make it even more effective. Here's an example of a personal e-mail message from a grantee to a funding representative at a foundation:

> *I thought of you as I opened the mail this morning to find the extraordinary news of a $60,000 gift from Jenny Jones. We mentioned your support of the expanding glaucoma screening initiative when we met with her, and I can't help but think that your support of our work in this area played a part in her generous decision to contribute. Thanks again!*
>
> Mary Smith
> Glaucoma Society

Think twice before asking a foundation program officer to read a lot of text via electronic media. Many nonprofits are issuing brochures, annual reports, and program updates in electronic format these days. These vehicles may meet the nonprofit's needs better than those of the foundation program officer. Building foundation engagement means putting their needs first and foremost in all communications. What follows is some advice along that score.

Ask yourself if you really think the foundation program officer has the time to download a large document. You would need to specify something of particular interest or make reference to the foundation and its page number in order to make this a valuable use of a foundation officer's time.

- The impact of an annual report or formal program update lies not only in its content but also in the quality of its design. Ask yourself if you want a program officer to print out pages and pages of your full-color carefully-designed-for-impact report, perhaps in black and white. Your organization should produce a limited supply of your glossy annual reports for foundation prospects and key donors. But keep in mind that the increasing numbers of foundations that require online proposals are often deeply committed to non-paper-based reports and communications for reasons of efficiency and to protect the environment. For those funders you probably *do* want to send everything electronically.

- Think more than twice before asking a program officer to look something up at a web site, by simply giving them a URL. If you consider it important for a funding representative to read a web page, watch a video, or access password-protected content, try to make that individual's life as easy it possible. It may be a good idea to create a hot button in the informing e-mail so that all the foundation program officer needs to do is click and be delivered to the appropriate web site.

4. Extraneous materials

Sending a DVD, CD, PowerPoint presentation, or anything that requires special equipment or software should only be done subsequent to a conversation with your program officer who has requested this item, or in adherence to the foundation's guidelines covering such matters. For some funders, for example, those that support the performing arts, this may be a common procedure. As a grantee, you should always ask in advance before sending along anything of this nature.

Selective cultivation activities

Meetings

The best cultivation meeting is one that is convened by the foundation at its offices or during a site visit at your organization. Your objective as a grantee should be to seek out every opportunity to meet personally with a funding representative. You should always mention your willingness or indeed eagerness to meet as part of:

• the proposal cover letter;

• the grant award thank-you letter;

• an e-mail or a personal note whenever some important "milestone" is reached during the grant period;

• a formal interim report or informal update on use of grant funds.

If you plan to highlight a grant-funded activity during your organization's board meeting, at a seasonal reception, or at a program out in the community, you should always invite your foundation program officer. Whether or not that individual attends, sends someone else, or just sends regrets, his or her experience will be a positive one, having noted that the program he or she funded is viewed as a high-priority item being showcased by your organization's leadership.

Publicity

If someone from your organization plans to do an op-ed piece, hold a press conference, give an interview to the media, or contribute to a feature article that covers the grant-funded activity, it's a good idea to give your funding representative a heads-up, well in advance, and to give that individual the opportunity to be included in any way that makes sense (maybe just by supplying a quote of some sort). Participation by your funder also carries the side benefit of enhancing the value of your piece to the publication in question, ensuring that it might actually get noticed and read by a larger audience.

Sometimes the more communication-minded grantmakers will issue their own press releases about your organization's grant, thereby creating a buzz on your behalf. Here's an example of a press release issued by the Raymond John Wean Foundation of Warren, Ohio, about two of its grantees:

FOR IMMEDIATE RELEASE

Contact:
Joel Ratner
President, The Raymond John Wean Foundation
330-394-3213

Dave Arnold
Family Service Agency
330-782-5664

Tim Schaffner
Valley Counseling Services Inc.
330-394-6244

Valley agencies combine resources for collaborative development project

Warren, Feb. 18, 2009 — With cuts in federal and state funding, Dave Arnold of Family Service Agency in Youngstown needed an employee to focus solely on development projects. Tim Schaffner of Valley Counseling Services, Inc. in Warren found himself in the same position — too many tasks to accomplish and not enough personnel or time.

The two decided to join their grant requests and share a development director between the two agencies. The Raymond John Wean Foundation noticed the collaborative spirit of their request and helped fund the development director position.

"It takes more than a year to reach a level of sustainability, and this is a great way to make that money last a lot longer," Schaffner said.

Supporting infrastructure improvements in the Mahoning Valley's nonprofit organizations is a large component of the work of the Wean Foundation. "They were really excited about a collaborative project," Arnold said.

With grant support from the Foundation, Schaffner and Arnold set to find a co-development director, sharing duties at both agencies. They hired Lindsay Molnar, a Trumbull County native returning to work in the Valley. "It's worked out really well. The agencies have similar objectives and its been interesting to learn what each agency offers," Molnar said.

After conducting her first foundation board meeting, Molnar will begin work on several goals for both agencies including searching for board members, writing grants and planning several major fundraising events.

"This is a step toward collaboration and affiliations that will benefit the client community," Arnold said.

"Their effort is a great example of how collaboration between agencies can work. Under this model we can better utilize our resources and more agencies benefit from grants," Ratner said.

For more information on this project please contact Joel Ratner, President of The Raymond John Wean Foundation, at 330-394-3213.

About The Raymond John Wean Foundation

The Raymond John Wean Foundation was created by Warren industrialist Raymond John "Jack" Wean in 1949. Annually, the Foundation gives approximately $4 million to nonprofit organizations with a majority of those funds earmarked for nonprofits in Mahoning and Trumbull Counties.

The mission of The Raymond John Wean Foundation is to enhance the community's well-being and vitality through grant making, convening, advocating and providing leadership with a focus on economically disadvantaged people and neighborhoods. Please visit www.rjweanfdn.org to learn more about the Foundation.

###

Events

If the nature of your grant project lends itself to some sort of opening reception or media event, be sure to include the foundation program officer appropriately, either as a guest speaker or as an individual to be recognized and thanked among the other VIPs in attendance. And if the nature of the funded activity includes lectures, symposia, seminars, or other gatherings where colleagues convene around issues related to the grant project, foundation program officers should be invited to join in or send a participant. In some instances they may even ask to invite another grantee working in the same subject field. Including these folks can only add to the level of the discussion, and acceptance by your foundation program officer is a clear sign that your organization's work is held in high regard by your funder.

Sometimes a chance encounter at someone else's event early on in the course of your grant project provides an opportunity for a conversation with a foundation program officer that not only includes your appreciation and an indication of how timely this grant is, but also a chance to query the foundation program officer as to what general communications they would like to receive. You could state that you look forward to keeping in touch with the program officer about the funded activity, but you want to be sure to do this in an appropriate manner. Would the program officer prefer to receive your print and/or e-newsletters and invitations to all events, or just select items having direct relevance to the program they are funding? The last thing you want to do, however, is to put your funding representative "on your mailing list" for all communiqués from your organization, especially if there are a lot of them. Most foundation program officers are grateful to be asked this question and will respond that they love to hear from their grantees, but hope that you will communicate "selectively." First asking the question and then behaving as requested reinforces the message that you are a responsible and considerate grantee.

Here are a few additional words of advice about communications that may seem like minor points but might prove useful:

- Final funding reports should always include the offer of photos of funded activity, if available, in any format the foundation requires. They may well decide to use them in their own reports, newsletters, and web site—excellent exposure for your organization.

- If your executive director, program director, or development officer managing the grantee/grantmaker relationship is invited to a symposium, reception, or other activity, and he or she knows it might interest your funding representative, as appropriate consider inviting that person to come along as a guest. And don't be worried about bringing your funder to an event where some other nonprofit organization is in the limelight. The more you treat your funding representative as a valued colleague, the greater the chances you yourself will be viewed that way.

We're all in this together

As a grantee you need to remember that foundation program officers and even the family members who serve as volunteer staff at some family foundations are working in environments not unlike that of your own organization. They too need to produce targeted communications for their stakeholders. They struggle with many of the same issues around communicating too much or too little and what formats to use to grab the attention of their desired audiences. They also appreciate the chance to network with colleagues in the field and enjoy participating in interesting meetings and events. When it comes to best practices in communication, there seems to be a genuine opportunity here to create a win/win situation for you and your funder.

5

Meetings With Funders

Stephanie Rapp

As in any good relationship, grantees and funders need some "face time." But how often, how long, and for what purpose is hard to gauge and will vary from foundation to foundation. Once you've received a first-time grant, chances are that your program officer has already done an initial site visit. And perhaps you've been to her office once or twice to discuss your proposal in its early stages.

After a grant has been awarded, the grantee and foundation program officer have the welcome opportunity for more honest communication, without the need to negotiate funding. Think about how to create opportunities for engaging meetings that allow you to demonstrate your agency's strengths; present voices of board members, clients, and colleagues; and demonstrate your value to the community you serve.

When will we meet again?

Here are some excellent reasons to invite your program officer for a follow-up visit:

1. Your organization has moved.

Whether it's down the block or across town, relocation is always a great excuse to extend an invitation. If you are a direct service provider, your venue is critical to your service delivery and will help form a clear picture in a program officer's mind of how you do business.

Whether you have already had a site visit or this is your program officer's first visit, these meetings are an integral part of the philanthropic process. Think about the impression you want to create. Some of the most compelling site visits for me have been to free clinics and social service agencies during their busiest times, when I have been able to witness first-hand the urgency of client needs. My first site visit to a free clinic that we ultimately supported was scheduled before the clinic doors opened. I can still picture the line of people waiting an hour or longer to ensure that they would be seen by the staff. Three years later, after our second grant had ended, I drove out to see the clinic in its new downtown location. Because of scheduling challenges, this visit was set for an evening when the clinic was closed. It was an informative but unemotional visit. Had I not already formed my initial strong impression, the second visit would have been less effective. Of course, key staff needs to be available during a site visit, hence the evening visit in my case. You don't want to interrupt vital services to impress a funder, but you do want funders to leave with a strong take-away.

If you are having a program officer visit you, I recommend sending them directions and a cell phone number if the meeting is off site. While many of us rely on the web to find meeting locations, those directions are not always accurate. I was once going to a site visit for a grantee that had moved, and I relied on the agency's web site to find its address. Unfortunately, its web site was not up to date and, after driving for an hour, I found myself on a dirt road in the middle of a cow pasture. It took a frantic phone call and another 20 minutes of driving before I landed in the right place. This made for a rushed visit and a more than slightly annoyed program officer.

Program officers don't get many opportunities to interact with the clients or beneficiaries of services offered by grantees. Think about how you can engage your clients in the site visit. If you are giving a first-time tour, solicit one or two clients to participate in the walk-through.

2. Your agency is marking an important milestone.

I have been surprised how often grantees hold significant events—a graduation for clients in a job training program, a prestigious award being presented to their executive director, an open house for the community—without sending an e-mail or invitation to our foundation. I'm not referring to the garden-variety fundraising dinners, which we do not generally attend, but significant events that would afford excellent opportunities to appreciate grantees in a more public setting. Chances are that your program officer may decline such invitations more often than not, but sending an invitation helps keep program officers posted on your activities, even if they cannot attend. Some program officers do not want to receive every public communication your agency sends out to its general list, but events are a good opportunity to shed extra light on your work.

3. You are preparing to, or have been invited to, apply for renewal funding.

If you are planning to request a renewal grant, a meeting to discuss your grant report is often useful. I ask grantees to allow me at least two and preferably four weeks after they send in their report (like most program officers, I have a lot of reports to read, approximately 60 each year) before we get together. A meeting gives us an opportunity to discuss their report and for me to pose questions, which I often do via e-mail in advance of our meeting so that the grantee can be as prepared as possible.

The conversation about a renewal grant is often more relaxed than the original meeting with a grantee (assuming you made good progress on your first grant), but you should be prepared to address honestly any challenges you experienced. Don't try to hide major problems that you encountered. Instead, think of how to present them as learning opportunities. Position a renewal request as a chance to build upon what you learned in the course of the prior year's grant. Funders like to leverage their investments. Helping you make course corrections is generally welcome, as long as you understand how to avoid the same challenges you might have encountered initially. If a grant has been particularly problematic, think about asking for a face-to-face meeting, rather than conveying difficult news by phone or e-mail. Under these circumstances bringing along one of your board members demonstrates that you have the backing of your organization's leadership, which can be useful if a program that was funded has not gone well.

4. Major staffing or leadership changes have taken place at your agency.

If a new executive director, or program manager, or anyone whose job is integral to the grant you've received has left your organization, it's always a good idea to invite your program officer to meet with that individual's successor, particularly if your funder knew the departing staffer well.

Again, think about including a seasoned board member or officer in this meeting, if you have someone who can speak with conviction and knowledge about the board's role in your organization. Foundation personnel don't often get to interact with board members of their grantee organizations, and such meetings can yield valuable insights into the leadership of an organization. This is particularly important if a new executive director has been appointed who has limited experience with the organization.

5. You are holding a conference, gathering, or other event.

Once I've made a grant, it's likely that the next time I'll see a representative of the grantee organization is at one of the grantee's events. I make a point of attending conferences, workshops, performances, and other programs organized by my grantees. I particularly like attending events where I can see the organization at work, meet some of its clients, see how staff and board present themselves, and observe the agency in a public setting. You may encounter foundation program officers who never show up for your events. If you do, don't take it personally. Whether they choose to participate or not, I still think it's a good idea to include them on your e-mail or invitation list, so that they are aware of what your agency is doing. I try to be unobtrusive at these gatherings. While I like to meet board members and clients, I don't like to be singled out and often try to find a seat in a location that makes it easy to slip out if I cannot stay for a full program.

Remember that funders are interested in the process, not just the outcomes, related to grants they award. For that reason, while inviting a program officer to the final performance of your arts education program might be interesting, it can be more revealing of your agency's work to invite her to a session where artists are mentoring students. Grantees often believe they need to show off only their most polished programs, but it is usually more illuminating for program officers to pull the curtain back and see how the actual work happens.

Since, as already noted, it can be helpful to you program officer to gain the perspectives of clients, partners, and participants in your organization's work, you should seek out opportunities to connect a program officer to these other voices. Can your clients or participants lead a tour or accompany a program officer on a site visit? Let the program officer have time alone with clients or constituents as well, so that they feel free to speak about their experiences without agency staff involved in the conversation.

The official site visit

I generally perform a site visit prior to making a grant, although this is not always possible with grantees located out of our area. But some foundations do not require a site visit as part of the grant decision-making process, and they may only do a visit at the conclusion of the grant, prior to considering a renewal. Some foundations don't do site visits at all. Still others visit all grantees. From my experience, an effective site visit sheds light on an organization in a way that is not possible through proposal review and other forms of due diligence.

Here is quick list of helpful items to consider when planning a site visit, no matter when during the grant cycle they occur:

- Arrange the visit for a time when you can show your agency off in the most favorable light. Think about not only when critical staff and board members will be available, but also when clients and community members may be accessing your services.

- Send clear and concise directions to your program officer, including parking and/or public transportation information. Provide a cell phone number if the visit is not at your primary location.

- Whenever possible, offer a tour, involving clients and/or participants. If that is not possible, try to have a client available during the site visit to talk with the program officer about their perspective on your services.

- Don't hand out materials and packets during the visit. You don't want your program officer rifling through papers when she needs to be observing your program in action and speaking with you and your team. Save those handouts as a take-away for the end of the meeting. If there are a lot of them, offer to mail them or send in e-format.

- If a previous grant from the foundation made possible something tangible (e.g., new equipment, a new roof, a publication), be sure to proudly display these during the visit.

- Be prepared to discuss current opportunities and challenges in an honest and open way. Since you have already received a grant, try not to focus on "selling" your organization, but rather think about illuminating and animating your agency's services in the context of community needs.

Here is a list of guidelines used by the Frances L. and Edwin L. Cummings Fund of New York, whose trustees perform site visits with grantees. This should provide you with important insights into the site visit from the funder's point of view.

**FOUNDATION
CENTER**
Knowledge to build on.

How to Approach a Foundation

What a Foundation Wants to Know
About Your Organization and Your Project

Guidelines for Meetings with Grantees from the
Frances L. and Edwin L. Cummings Fund

- Is the Executive Director an effective leader with a capable and well-trained staff?

- Does the organization have a proven track record in general? Specifically as to this program?

- Does this organization have the capability of expanding to meet the community's increasing needs?

- Is this organization offering innovative programs or is it replicating other's efforts?

- What is the overall present financial situation of this organization?

- Is the Board of Directors an "active" or a "paper" Board?

- Does the Board financially support the organization commensurate with their means?

- Do they also solicit support from their personal/business contacts?

- Does the organization have a written long range plan and mission statement developed with the full participation of the Board?

Some topics to consider raising during the site visit include:

- Have there been any major changes at the organization that your program officer should be made aware of? This includes staffing and board, or venue.

- What significant milestones have occurred: favorable publicity (bring copies of articles), gain or loss of major funding, awards bestowed, new programs or collaborations? All of these changes are opportunities to reinforce your program officer's knowledge of and familiarity with your organization.

- Is there important research or information about your field that has just been or is about to be released? Program officers are eager to stay on top of their fields and are always looking for sources of current data and studies. If you are able to supply your program officer with such breaking news, it will make you stand out.

- Are you engaging in a strategic or other planning or assessment process? If there is a long-standing relationship with a grantee, I have found it useful to participate in the strategic planning process. This might involve a meeting with a board member or consultant, or just being available to answer a few questions by phone.

At whatever point in the proposal review/grant award/renewal consideration process your funder conducts a site visit, keep in mind that the impressions your program officer gains about your organization by means of this meeting go a long way toward determining whether or not you receive a grant, how much you receive, and whether or not you receive follow-up funding.

At the end of this chapter is a staff assessment form used by the Salem Health & Wellness Foundation of Salem, Oregon, for their board docket. You will note the site visit mentioned on page 2, along with the ratings for the strength of the proposal. A number of these items are best ascertained during a face-to-face meeting between funder and grantee or prospective grantee.

Final words

It's important to remember that, at its core, a successful funding relationship, like any other relationship, is about building trust and a sense of comfort and camaraderie between key staff and the foundation program officer. With the ease and convenience of voice mail and e-mail, grantees today are able to stay in touch quickly and have questions answered with relative ease. Meetings are a more deliberate and intentional opportunity to present information about your agency, so be sure to use your face time wisely.

DOCKET & STAFF ASSESSMENT

SALEM HEALTH & WELLNESS FOUNDATION

Proposal #:

Organization Name:
City:
Purpose of project:
Need Addressed:
Requested Amount:
Duration of grant period:

REVIEW SUMMARY:	SATISFACTORY	UNSATISFACTORY	UNCLEAR	N/A
Addresses SHWF areas of interest	☐	☐	☐	☐
Organizational Capacity	☐	☐	☐	☐
Financial Stability	☐	☐	☐	☐
Community Recognition and Support	☐	☐	☐	☐
Project Likelihood of Success	☐	☐	☐	☐

PAST GRANT ACTIVITY:

Achieved goals specified when previously supported by SHWF?   ☐ **YES**   ☐ **NO**
If no, please explain.

COMPLIANCE ASSESSMENT:

OK

		Comments
	Name and address of organization	
	Contact person(s) and title(s)	
	Executive Director or President	
	Phone, fax, and e-mail provided by applicant	
	Narrative Statement summarizing the proposal	
	Meets geographic area requirements of SHWF	
	The total annual organizational budget for current fiscal year	
	The total project budget	
	The dollar amount requested	
	Indirect costs less than 10% of total grant request	
	Equipment costs less than 30% of total costs	
	Bio sketch, C.V. or resume of principals	
	Journal articles, etc. evidencing proposed services or interventions represent "best practices".	

COMPLIANCE ASSESSMENT (con't):

OK   **Comments**

	Proof of non-profit status - 501(c)(3) IRS Determination letter	
	Signature of approving personnel	
	No. of copies (at least 10)	
	Two most recent audits or Form 990	
	Requires exercise of Right of First Opportunity	
	Other: _____	

Conducted:

☐ Site Visit

☐ Pre-application Meeting with Organization

☐ Other:

SHWF RELATIONSHIPS:

PROPOSAL STRENGTH:

	SATISFACTORY	UNSATISFACTORY	UNCLEAR	N/A
Addresses a clear and important need in a realistic way	☐	☐	☐	☐
Goals/objectives/time frame defined with a strategy for achieving results	☐	☐	☐	☐
Adequate number of qualified staff	☐	☐	☐	☐
Leads to long-term solutions	☐	☐	☐	☐
Potential for collaboration with other organizations/funders	☐	☐	☐	☐
Impact on target audience(s)	☐	☐	☐	☐
Request reasonable in light of the Foundation's resources	☐	☐	☐	☐
Proposal leverages other financial resources	☐	☐	☐	☐
Organization can support project in the future	☐	☐	☐	☐

| Organization's mission linked to request | ☐ | ☐ | ☐ | ☐ |

COMMENTS ON PROPOSAL STRENGTH:

FINANCIAL STABILITY OF ORGANIZATION:

	SATISFACTORY	UNSATISFACTORY	UNCLEAR	N/A
Adequate funding at present	☐	☐	☐	☐
Reasonable funding plan	☐	☐	☐	☐
Private funding received annually	☐	☐	☐	☐
Public funding received annually	☐	☐	☐	☐
Organization leverages resources through collaboration and partnership	☐	☐	☐	☐

COMMENTS ON FINANCIAL STABILITY:

EVALUATION PLAN:

	SATISFACTORY	UNSATISFACTORY	UNCLEAR	N/A
Data Collection Process	☐	☐	☐	☐
Measureable outcomes	☐	☐	☐	☐
Intermediate and long term outcomes	☐	☐	☐	☐
Plan to measure and monitor success/impact	☐	☐	☐	☐

COMMENTS ON EVALUATION PLAN:

STAFF COMMENTS:

6

Lessons Learned

Sidney R. Hargro

Introduction

"Follow effective action with quiet reflection. From the quiet reflection will come even more effective action."

Peter F. Drucker

Arguably, the most critical step in the program delivery and fund development process happens after the funds are procured. It involves monitoring program delivery and outcome measures that enable the nonprofit to continuously improve programming and periodically report back to stakeholders. Although fund development staff typically do not handle this activity, strategic attention to measures throughout the program year will produce both the qualitative and quantitative information needed to develop a strong case for ongoing financial support from public funding sources, foundations, and individual donors. Once program measures are established, the case for continued support is strengthened by an increased ability to:

- Explain discrepancies between actual and projected program performance results and proactively address how the gap might be closed;

- Assess results and identify if an achieved level of performance can be improved upon and show stakeholders a commitment to continuous improvement;

- Exchange ongoing feedback among everyone involved in achieving results (e.g., intake, program participants, program staff, volunteers) by reviewing progress periodically, reinforcing activities that achieve results, and intervening to address issues where needed.

This chapter will explore:

- The importance of having a culture of learning

- How to develop a data collection plan

- Choosing a performance management data systems

- Sharing lessons learned

- Getting started

Additionally, the chapter concludes with a case study of one nonprofit's experience integrating a learning culture and robust processes for determining lessons learned.

Importance of having a culture of learning

In his book *Developing a Learning Culture in Nonprofit Organizations*, human performance consultant Stephen J. Gill explains that a learning culture is produced when an organization makes reflection, feedback, and knowledge sharing part of the way it operates its business daily. This is not easily accomplished, since it requires that the key attributes of a learning organization be ingrained in the culture and embraced at all levels of operation. Five known attributes of learning organizations are:

- *Systematic problem solving*—Insisting on use of data to diagnose problems and make decisions

- *Experimentation*—Searching for and testing new knowledge by testing ideas without fear of failing

- *Learning from past experience*—Periodically reviewing both successes and failures to record lessons learned

- *Learning from others*—Benchmarking or learning from others in the field to ensure that best practices are uncovered

- *Transferring knowledge*—Cross-functional sharing of knowledge throughout the organization.[1]

Although it is difficult to embrace all five attributes, nonprofits can set the tone that these attributes are important and that "learning from results" is everyone's job. Achieving these attributes removes the identification of lessons learned from the singular purview of program and evaluation staff and takes full advantage of an organization's skill, experience, and knowledge base. An example will be found in the nonprofit case study at the end of the chapter.

---

[1]Garvin, David A. "Building a Learning Organization." Harvard Business Review 71, no. 4 (July–August 1993): 78–91.

How to develop a data collection plan

Driven by the reporting requirements of funders, many grantees view external impact or outcome measurement as the be-all and end-all metric in monitoring, reporting, and gauging success. During the grant application process, grantees typically are asked to develop an evaluation plan that will indicate program impact at the end of the grant period. These measures are lagging or retrospective indicators. Although technically this may fulfill the required evaluation responsibility identified in the grant agreement, it is insufficient to identify lessons learned and ultimately problematic for the sustainability of the program. This fallacy of outcome measurement makes nonprofits overlook the very operational drivers that caused the results. To alleviate this problem, nonprofits should develop a more comprehensive data collection plan that identifies and links both operational performance measures, which are leading or predictive indicators that monitor the delivery of the program, and outcome measures.

Once performance goals are determined, nonprofits should select the simplest, most practical data collection method needed to continuously improve programming and adequately report outcomes and lessons learned. All nonprofits regardless of size and available resources should collect both program delivery and outcome measures. Figure 6-1 shows a table of qualitative and quantitative program delivery and outcome measures.

Figure 6-1. Program Delivery and Outcome Measures

	Qualitative	Quantitative
Delivery	• How well the program is being delivered (e.g., attendance, completion) • Client satisfaction with program delivery • Direct observation (of program delivery by staff) • Organizational records	• Number of client interactions • Duration of client interactions • Cost-benefit analysis (paying for success) • Client activity log
Outcome	• Client self-reported stories regarding level of success (e.g., exit survey) • Client stories depicting the path from pre-program period issue to post-program period successes • Direct observation (of client)	• Amount, degree of success of individual client and/or aggregate group of clients (e.g., 80 percent achieved a successful result) • Benchmark comparison

Similarly, program delivery and outcome measures should include both qualitative and quantitative measures. In a Bridgespan Group case study of the Great Valley Center in Modesto, California, Don Howard and Susan J. Colby referred to this multi-method approach as:

> …an essential aspect of performance measurement, stating that quantitative measurement of performance [Hargro: *should never*] take the place of [Hargro: *client*] "stories." While it may be tempting (at least for some) to try to reduce the performance of a nonprofit organization to sterile facts and figures, what draws most of us (nonprofit leaders, staff, and funders) to the social sector is a passion to improve the lives of real people. As such, it's critically important to stay in touch with how the organization's work affects the people it serves.[2]

Once a data collection plan has been developed and integrated into the work of the nonprofit, results should be monitored immediately for noteworthy trends. This will uncover issues that need to be addressed and improve chances of success.

Example:

> A comprehensive study of Columbus City Schools, an urban public school district in Columbus, Ohio, revealed that students who moved two or more times were more likely to experience a negative impact in their academic performance. Additionally, the more stable students that were a part of highly mobile school populations were also adversely impacted. To address this issue, an entrepreneurial philanthropist funded a mobility prevention coordinator position in a middle school building that was found to experience one of the highest levels of mobility.
>
> The coordinator designed a data collection plan that included quantitative measures regarding students that left the program and qualitative measures from exit interviews. After a few months of collecting and monitoring the data, it was clear that many students who changed residences (but wanted to stay at the same school) were not taking advantage of a district policy that offered transportation back to the school of origin as long as the new residence was within a defined radial distance (regardless of the assigned school for their new residence).
>
> With the benefit of a good but simple data collection plan, the coordinator uncovered this issue midway through the first program year—early enough to intervene by alerting parents and the transportation department. This intervention was pivotal in helping the program significantly reduce student mobility at the middle school in the first year. Thus, regular and ongoing monitoring matters and can place the nonprofit in a position to improve chances for achieving outcome goals by the end of the program year.

[1]Howard, Don and Susan J. Colby. "Great Valley Center: A Case Study in Measuring for Mission." *The Bridgespan Group*. 1 December 2003. (www.bridgespan.org/learningcenter/resourcedetail.aspx?id=422).

Choosing a performance management data system

The goal of performance management is to ensure that the organization and all of the subsystems that are required to deliver the program (e.g., outreach, recruitment, program delivery) are working together in an optimum fashion that places the organization in the best position to achieve the desired results. In order to collect, manage, and share the information in reports, nonprofits must consider what software they will use to house and maintain their data.

For many nonprofits, Microsoft Excel is an adequate solution, and it is widely used for developing dashboards and scorecards.[3] An Excel-based workbook can be developed that links related data by program and relation to operational objectives. However, the more complex the service delivery processes are for a nonprofit, the more likely it is that use of basic software such as Microsoft Excel will not adequately suit their needs.

The National Technology Network (NTEN), a national membership organization of nonprofit technology professionals, uses Microsoft Excel to track weekly indicators, calculate monthly indicators, show graphical presentations of how the data measures up against organizational goals year-to-date, and display a graphical summary of how the measures compare to the same time period in the previous year.[4] See Figure 6-2 for an example screenshot by NTEN.

Figure 6-2. A Screenshot of a Weekly and Monthly Summary of Data

WEEKLY SUMMARY

MEMBERSHIP	3-Apr-09	10-Apr-09
NEW Joins for WEEK	30	30
NEW Renewals for WEEK	30	30
TOTAL MEMBERSHIPS	840	900
Individuals Receiving Member Benefits	1,680	1,800
# of Individuals per Organization Membership	2.50	2.50

EVENTS / MEMBERSHIP	3-Apr-09	10-Apr-09
TOTAL Memberships w 1+ Registration	200	200
% of Memberships w 1+ Registration	23.81%	22.22%

RENEWALS	3-Apr-09	10-Apr-09
Total Renewals (Oct-Sep)	1,122	1,130
Total Unrenewed	78	70
TOTAL RENEWAL RATE	93.54%	94.19%

WEBSITE ANALYTICS (Main Site)	3-Apr-09	10-Apr-09
# of Visits in Past Week	1,000	1,000
Avg. Time on Site	01:00	01:00
Pages / Visit	2.00	2.00
# Visits YTD	14,000	15,000
Avg. Time on Site YTD	01:00	01:00
Pages / Visit YTD	2.00	2.00

WEBINARS	3-Apr-09	10-Apr-09
# of Webinars YTD	14	15
# of Registrants YTD	280	300
Average Attendance YTD	20.00	20.00
# of Recordings Viewed YTD	140	150

Yearly Conference	3-Apr-09	10-Apr-09
# of Registrations in Past Week	200	200
Registrants w Member Benefits	100	100
Registrants w/o Member Benefits	100	100
Cancellations	10	10
TOTAL REGISTRANTS	2660	2850

MONTHLY SUMMARY

MEMBERSHIP	Feb-09	Mar-09
Total Joins (Jan-Dec)	600	900
Goal for Total Joins (Jan-Dec)	600	900
% of Goal	100.00%	100.00%
Total Renewals (Oct-Sep)	1,500	1,800
Goal for Total Renewals (Oct-Sep)	1,500	1,800
% of Goal	100.00%	100.00%
TOTAL MEMBERSHIPS	1,200	1,800
GOAL FOR TOTAL MEMBERSHIPS	1,200	1,800
% of Goal	100.00%	100.00%
TOTAL Membership Revenue YTD	$6,000.00	$9,000.00
Yearly Membership Revenue Goal	$6,000.00	$9,000.00
% of Goal	100.00%	100.00%
Individuals Receiving Member Benefits	1,000	1,000
# of Individuals per Organization Membership	0.75	0.33

EVENTS / MEMBERSHIP	Feb-09	Mar-09
TOTAL Memberships w 1+ Registration	200	200
% of Memberships w 1+ Registration	16.67%	11.11%

WEBSITE ANALYTICS (Main Site)	Feb-09	Mar-09
# of Visits in Past Month	500	1,000
% Increase from Previous Year	0.00%	0.00%
Avg. Time on Site	02:00	01:00
% Increase from Previous Year	0.00%	0.00%
Pages / Visit	2.00	2.00
% Increase from Previous Year	0.00%	0.00%
# Visits YTD	1,500	2,500
% Increase from Previous Year	0.00%	0.00%
Avg. Time on Site YTD	01:20	01:12
% Increase from Previous Year	0.00%	0.00%
Pages / Visit YTD	2.00	2.00
% Increase from Previous Year	0.00%	0.00%

AFFINITY GROUPS	Feb-09	Mar-09
Active Users	1,000	1,000
Total Users	2,000	2,000
New Users	0	0
Total Groups	100	100
Total Messages	10,000	10,000
New Messages	0	0

WEBINARS	Feb-09	Mar-09
# of Webinars YTD	20	30
# of Registrants YTD	200	300
Average Attendance YTD	10.00	10.00
Webinar Revenue YTD	$2,000.00	$3,000.00
Yearly Revenue Goal	$2,000.00	$3,000.00
% of Goal	100.00%	100.00%

Yearly Conference	Feb-09	Mar-09
# of Registrations in Past Week	110	110
Registrants w Member Benefits	100	100
Registrants w/o Member Benefits	10	10
Cancellations	1	1
TOTAL REGISTRANTS	218	327
NTC Revenue YTD	$8,000.00	$12,000.00

NEWSLETTER	Feb-09	Mar-09
Subscription Total	1,000	1,000
New Subscriptions	0	0
Subscription Goal	1,000	1,000
% of Goal	100.00%	100.00%

[3]An explanation from TDWI's "Deploying Dashboards and Scorecards": "The primary difference between dashboards and scorecards is that dashboards tend to monitor the performance of operational processes [Hargro: *or program delivery in the case of nonprofits*] whereas scorecards tend to chart the progress toward tactical and strategic goals. Dashboards also tend to display charts and tables, whereas scorecards use graphical symbols and icons [Hargro: *e.g., red, yellow, green traffic lights*] to represent the status and trends of key metrics." (Eckerson, Wayne W. "Deploying Dashboards and Scorecards." *TDWI Best Practices Report*. July 2006. TDWI. <download.101com.com/pub/tdwi/Files/RRS_DB_Q206_F_web.pdf>.), p 9.

[4]Hedstrom, Karl. "Dashboards: Track Your Organizational Progress." *Nonprofit Technology Network* (NTEN). 16 April 2009. (nten.org/blog/2009/04/16/dashboards-track-your-organizational-progress).

More extensive performance data systems for nonprofits are available from software developers CiviCore (www.civicore.com), Social Solutions (www.socialsolutions. com), and nFocus (www.nfocus.com), among others. The cost of these systems, however, may be prohibitive for small- to mid-sized nonprofit organizations.

Regardless of which data system a nonprofit chooses, it is important for it to be well designed with all stakeholders in mind. As mentioned earlier, developing a useful system will lend itself to not only more effective service to clients but also an enhanced ability to build a case for continuous improvement in an increasingly competitive market.

Sharing lessons learned

Nonprofit organizations should communicate simple, compelling, and meaningful developments, outcomes, and lessons learned with all stakeholders, including trustees, foundations, donors, and advocates, on a regular basis to share and emphasize the importance of their work. Grants, donations, volunteered time, pro bono services, etc. are all stakeholder investments, and as a general rule those who provide them should receive information regarding relevant milestones or results regarding programs they support. Although preference for regular communication depends on the stakeholder, bi-monthly to quarterly communication is usually adequate.

Figure 6-3 and Figure 6-4 are two examples of simple funder e-mail communications submitted by the director of the Father to Father parenting program at the Columbus Urban League.

Figure 6-3. Example of Funder E-mail Communication

Greetings:

As a supporter of the Columbus Urban League's African American Male Initiative (AAMI) Father to Father program we are inviting you to be our guest at our fourth graduation. The fathers in this program have completed a 12-week curriculum designed to assist them in overcoming the barriers that prevent them from being the fathers they desire to be. This ceremony will take place Wednesday April 29, 2009 in the Columbus Urban League multi-purpose room. Food and Beverages will be provided.

Our next class begins on Tuesday, May 26 from 10 am to 12:30 pm and Thursday, May 28 from 6 pm to 8:30 pm.

Glenn A. Harris
Director—A.A.M.I

Figure 6-4. Example of Funder E-mail Communication

Greetings:

As one of our key supporters, we are inviting you to the next African American Male Initiative (AAMI) Father to Father program workshop that we use to inform the community and recruit fathers to our program:

"How to Navigate the Child Support System"

Participants in the workshop will also be introduced to our more intensive 12-week Father to Father program.

1060 Mt. Vernon Avenue
May 22, 2009
3–5 p.m.

Glenn A. Harris
Director–AAMI

Asking stakeholders in what format and how much information they would like to receive is a normal part of building a network of advocates for nonprofits. Not all stakeholders should receive the same communications, nor should they all receive all communications. Nonprofits can also test the receptivity of constituents by sending out communication vehicles and asking stakeholders to opt in or opt out.

Communication of lessons learned and program impact can be accomplished in a variety of ways, including through e-mails, text messages, posts on social networking sites such as Twitter and Facebook, formal letters, e-newsletters, updates on the nonprofit's web site, and more. For example, periodic e-mails to funders depicting the progress and impact of their support will keep the program top-of-mind and ultimately help make the case for additional funding. Also, regular communication about lessons learned to volunteers can inspire them to invite others in their spheres of influence to become volunteers and advocates as well.

Getting started

Developing a learning organizational culture and adequate performance measure systems cannot be achieved overnight. In fact, it can be argued that becoming a learning organization that uses data to make decisions and communicate results to constituents is not a destination or status to be achieved but rather an evolutionary path that leads nonprofits continuously toward better outcomes for their clients, community, and supporters.

It is very easy to get lost in planning and discussion of minutiae regarding how, when, and where to begin and the organization's capacity to engage in continuous performance measurement. Empower a cross-functional team of staff to begin reviewing organizational practices and identifying what they believe to be the most meaningful measures to track. Compare this to data from the field that is important and meaningful to the success of similar programs. Consider involving funders and other stakeholders in the development of a communications plan that will share your lessons learned. Then, set up a data collection and management system and get started.

A Case Study in Embracing Lessons Learned

Ohio Association of Second Harvest Food Banks—Ohio Benefit Bank program

Executive Director: Lisa Hamler-Fugitt
Location: Columbus, Ohio
Target Audience: Ohio (rural and urban area communities)
Staff Size: 20
Budget: $12 million

Background:

The Ohio Association of Second Harvest Foodbanks (OASHF) is a nonprofit based in Columbus, Ohio that assists designated Second Harvest Foodbanks throughout Ohio in providing food and other resources to people in need. According to their nonprofit portrait on PowerPhilanthropy.org, Ohio Benefit Bank program (OBB), Ohio's affiliate of The Benefit Bank project offered by the National Council of Churches, the Jewish Council on Public Affairs, and several other national organizations OASHF, "is an Internet-based program that facilitates free tax filing for both state and federal taxes and screens families for potential eligibility for work support benefits. In its third year of operation, over 850 sites have been established and over 3,000 counselors have been trained in nearly all of Ohio's counties."

Organizational Culture:

"There are no mistakes here, only lessons learned." At OASHF, this old adage is a way of doing business. From the executive director, Lisa Hamler-Fugitt to program management to line staff to call operators, this philosophy permeates

---

[5]"Nonprofit Portrait: Ohio Association of Second Harvest Foodbanks." PowerPhilanthropy.org. The Columbus Foundation. (https://powerphilanthropy.org/viewPublicReport.do?organizationId=1016678, www.bridgespan.org/learningcenter/resourcedetail. aspx?id=422).

the culture and organically creates buy-in from staff and increasing support from constituents.

Jason Elchert, the Director of Outreach and Education for the Ohio Benefit Bank program, says that "staff has become accustomed to sitting down cross-functionally as a team—it's just the way we operate." As they collect data on the program, staff members discuss the results as a team to determine if there is something that should be addressed or a trend that needs to be monitored.

Data Collection Plan:

The data collection plan for the Ohio Benefit Bank begins the moment a call is received and triaged by operators. In addition to basic information on the client, the intake process includes collecting detailed information on the presenting problem by asking the following nine "yes" or "no" questions:

- Are you working?

- Are you receiving unemployment compensation?

- Have you or another member of your household been laid off in the past 12 months?

- Did you apply for unemployment?

- Did you receive unemployment?

- Have you or another household member exhausted your unemployment benefits without finding another job?

- Is your home currently in foreclosure?

- Are your utilities shut off or have you received a disconnect notice?

- How are you coping?

The last question, "How are you coping?" offers the following seven multiple-choice answers:

❏ Check cashing/payday loan service

❏ Rent-to-own furniture or appliances

❏ Borrowing money or food from family and friends

❏ Selling personal items on eBay, Craigslist, yard sale, or pawn shop

❏ Moved in with family or friends

❑ Selling blood or plasma

❑ Other

This information is used to inform internal process, intervention strategy, and overall client service. OASHF typically does not share this information with funders or other stakeholders. However, as Figure 6-5 shows, OASHF prepares impact data monthly, quarterly, and annually.

Figure 6-5. OASHF Impact Data

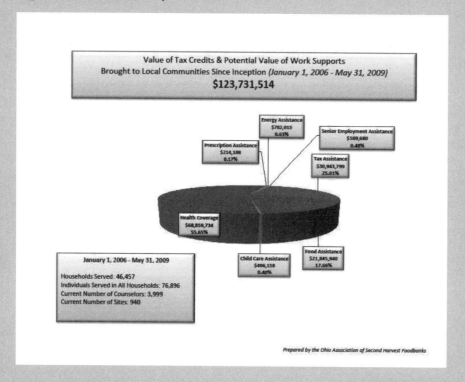

These measures are regularly shared with all of OASHF funders and stakeholders to keep them abreast of the "social return" on their charitable and public investment. By adding to this a breakdown of benefits received by family size and anecdotal client stories, OASHF has the ability to monitor both the service delivery and impact of the Ohio Benefit Bank and make real-time changes to their programming to assure continuous improvement.

Performance Management Data System:

OASHF is a steadily expanding nonprofit organization with a current annual budget of over $12 million. Until this year, OASHF has used only Microsoft Excel to collect data. However, due to the major expansion experienced over the last few years, they recently purchased the Social Solutions ETC (Efforts to Outcomes) product. They believe that

The Grant Report

Nancy Wiltsek

Background

The number of private foundations hovers around 72,000. Google the term "grant report" and you get a staggering 50 million-plus results. Those very large numbers belie the fact that the majority of foundations do not require formal grant reports (the majority don't require or accept proposals either). However, assuming you're reading this book and this chapter, you have been funded by at least one foundation that does both.

For those foundations that employ staff and/or make larger grants, chances are they will have at least minimal reporting requirements. Others may expect a full-fledged external evaluation. Regardless of where they are on the continuum, the vast majority will have their own unique formats and requirements. After hearing the news that a grant was approved, the most important thing a grant recipient needs to know is what that funder's reporting rules are.

Grant reports are the vehicles of choice for collecting a vast array of grant-related information, and they can serve both the grantmaker and the grant recipient. At the most basic level, funders want to know how their money was spent and the effect the grant had on the people and issues they care about. For some, the report is simply a tool for financial accountability to ensure the grant was spent as intended. For others, the report is designed to focus on outcomes, the impact of the grant or the positive change toward which the grant contributed. Still others may ask about lessons learned, organizational changes, or what challenges are coming down the pike—either in the field in which you work, or for the organization itself.

The issue of organizational capacity and effectiveness is one in which many funders are very interested. They want to know how the organization works and what challenges the organization may be facing. It's important to understand that funders do not make these requests to ferret out weaknesses for the purpose of punishment, but rather so that they might help the grantee with anything from advice to additional financial support for relevant capital expenditures, technical assistance, consulting, etc.

Honesty is both critical and expected when reporting to your funder. In fact, candid responses will often deepen the relationship between grantor and grantee, and may even result in additional financial support to address a problem strategically. Other reasons that foundations require reports include the fact that they often have their own internal goals, objectives, and strategies; thus their ability to assess their success is dependent on their ability to assess their grantees' success. And foundations increasingly are utilizing electronic grants management systems, which track all aspects of the grantmaking process and for which a final report provides administrative closure for the grant.

The grant report can serve the grantee partner as well. Rather than being a burden, preparing and submitting a report enables the organization to reflect on what was achieved over the grant period and what changes, if any, might be made to improve programs and results moving forward, and to communicate to the grantmaker the important work the organization is doing and how it is making a difference in the world. Thus the grant report provides a chance to tell the story to the funder(s) who helped make the work possible. It is also an opportunity to communicate gratitude and enable the funder to better understand the success, and challenges, of the organization and its work.

An informal survey I conducted of family foundations in mid-2009 found that:

- All required a report (narrative and financial);
- All informed their grantees of reporting requirements and due dates as part of the grant agreement letter;
- All accepted hard-copy reports, although some accept them by e-mail or via their web sites if they have an online grants management system; and
- Nearly all had information about reporting requirements on their web sites.

All had their own report forms as well. The idiosyncratic nature of foundations is one of the biggest challenges in grant reporting. It is incumbent upon the nonprofit grantee to understand what the funder expects and to be clear, and honest, about what the nonprofit can deliver. Reporting requirements are best discussed right after the grant has been approved and, in many cases, will be included in the grant agreement letter or can be found on the funder's web site. Ideally the funder will provide guidance and/or a grant report form that will specify exactly what is expected, as well as due dates for interim and final reports. If there is no verbal communication from the program officer or written information in the grant agreement letter about reporting requirements, by all means ask!

In many cases, the type of grant (project support, general operating support, capacity building, capital expenditure, etc.) will determine the scope of the report. For example, reporting on a grant for direct services might focus on how many people were served and to what extent lives or circumstances were improved. A report on a general operating support grant might focus on progress toward larger organizational goals to advance a social change agenda. A report for a capacity-building grant might focus on how the funds were used to help strengthen the organization. And a grant report on capital expenditure might focus on how the purchase or renovation made expansion of services possible.

There are three general types of grant reports:

- An **interim grant report** is used as a mid–grant period check-in to ensure that things are going as planned. If not, the interim report enables the grantee to share any problems or issues that may require a change in the grant objectives or grant agreement. It is imperative that issues be communicated honestly so that mid-year corrections can be made, if necessary.

- A **multi-year grant report** is for grants that will be paid in installments over a period of time (usually two, three, or five years). A report is submitted at the end of each grant year and, in most cases, must be received and reviewed before additional installments of the grant money will be released.

- A **final grant report** addresses all plans or goals and objectives stated in the grant proposal. For the most part this chapter deals with final grant reports, although much of the information is relevant to interim and multi-year reports as well.

Grant report basics

A successful grant report has much in common with a successful grant proposal. As the proposal was undoubtedly well organized and succinctly described the purpose for which the funds would be used, who would be served, and what would be accomplished, the grant report should be well organized and succinctly describe how the funds were used, who was served, and what was accomplished. More often than not, the grant proposal can serve as a guide for the grant report.

Grant report components: In general, grant reports should be submitted with a cover sheet or cover letter and have two sections: the narrative and the financial. In some cases, additional information may be requested by the funder.

Cover sheet

If the foundation uses a grant report form, it will often provide a cover sheet, which can be downloaded from the funder's web site. Cover sheets tend to follow a standard format and are used to collect basic information, such as organization name, project name, grant amount, date of grant, and contact information. If there is no cover sheet, you should have a cover letter addressed to the appropriate foundation representative. The cover letter is a good place to express your gratitude for the grant and highlight one or two successes made possible by the funder's support.

Narrative

The narrative part of the report should be a concise and well-written piece that tells the reader what happened over the course of the grant period. If a report format or list of questions is provided by the funder, the report should follow it exactly. (Often information is requested in a particular order so that it can be downloaded into a foundation's grants management software program or compared with other data.) If your proposal listed specific goals and objectives, be sure your report addresses each one (again, your proposal can serve as a guide for your report). If an objective was not met, state what progress was made, and your best assessment as to why the effort fell short of expectations. Ignoring an unmet objective raises a red flag to the reader; it is better to address it openly and honestly.

Financial report

The financial report describes how the funds were spent. If the proposal stated that funds would be used for specific line items, the report should show that. If the funds were given for general operating expenses, a statement of revenue and expenses may suffice. Assuming you are using standard budgeting software, reports should be easy to generate and should be acceptable to the funder. To be safe, if a financial report form is not provided, ask the foundation what format is preferred.

Additional information/attachments

Additional information can include anything from case studies to videos, photos, news clippings, annual reports, research reports, etc. This is where you can portray the human story about the work you're doing. If additional information is relevant and can complement the story you're trying to tell, then send it along, but be discerning. Funders do not want or need vast amounts of extraneous material to wade through.

What do funders really want to know?

Below are sample questions culled from a number of different foundation report forms that you might find in the narrative section of a grant report. (Note that typically these questions would be answered in three to five pages.)

1. Please give a brief description of the project/program supported by the foundation (if the grant was for general operating expenses, describe how grant funds were used).

2. Please describe the *impact* the program/organization has had on the population served. What is different as a result of the work? Please discuss qualitative positive change and/or outcomes in addition to numbers served.

3. Was the program implemented as described in the original grant proposal? Were the original program objectives achieved or exceeded? If not, please explain.

4. With 20/20 hindsight, is there anything you might have done differently, or is there anything you learned that will change the program/organization in the future?

5. Did the organization encounter a change in leadership or a significant management challenge over the course of the year? If so, how was it addressed?

As just one example, here are the Fan Fox and Leslie R. Samuels Foundation, Inc.'s reporting requirements (a formal presentation is also required):

FINAL REPORT

The Final Report is due after the Final Presentation (guidelines for the Final Presentation will be provided towards the end of the grant term). The content of the Final Report differs slightly from that of the Interim Reports, although the format is similar. It may be up to 15 pages of text, and should cover the <u>entire</u> grant period and all grant related activities.

REPORT CHECKLIST

Report includes:
- ❑ Title Page including: Program name, dates covered by this report, Program Director name(s), address, telephone, email, and report submission date.
- ❑ Written Report
- ❑ Financial Reports
  - ▪ Final Grant Financial Report (signed)
  - ▪ Total Program Financial Report (signed)
  - ▪ Financial Narrative
- ❑ Updated Pro Forma

REPORT SECTIONS

I. Background
Restate the original goals and objectives of the Program as proposed and explain any changes that have occurred over the course of the grant period. Briefly describe the context in which the Program was developed and your original estimation of its impact. If any changes in circumstances have altered the context or potential impact, please explain these.

II. Grant Summary of Results
Include a separate page, in the format below which provides a summary of the grant.

GRANT SUMMARY OF RESULTS
Organization, Department
Program Director
Grant Dates

Projected	Actual
Goal 1	
Objective 1	
Objective 2	
Goal 2	
Objective 1	
Objective 2	
Goal 3	
Objective 1	
Objective 2	
# of Patients/Clients Served	
Total Program Cost	
Samuels Foundation Grant Budget	Note any major line item disparities
Model of Sustainability	
Plan or Potential for Replication/Dissemination	

III. Program Implementation and Administration

This section should summarize what you learned over the course of the implementation. If you encountered particularly difficult, interesting or unique problems during the implementation of the Program, please describe them and how they were resolved. This information will help us assist future grantees in similar situations.

IV. Final Outcomes

Focus on the goals you have achieved and challenges you met during the entire grant period. List any programs or products that resulted from this grant and summarize any data you collected. Describe any new knowledge or ideas you formed about the issues examined and the conclusions that can be drawn from the Program. Results from evaluations and data analysis should be used in the discussion to support these conclusions. Please provide the data regarding the number of people affected by your program (see chart below). Also, provide a description of how each category of participant was impacted by the Program.

USE THE CATEGORIES OF YOUR FINAL PRESENTATION

Category	Goal for Grant Period	Cumulative from Inception to End of Reporting Period
Patients/Clients		
Professionals, by type, (Physician, Social Workers, etc.)		
Non-professionals (e.g. family members, care givers)		

V. Future Plans and Dissemination

Describe what activities will continue and the infrastructure in place to facilitate continued activities. Tell us how the Program has become self-sustaining or will receive funds from other sources in the future.

Discuss your plans for dissemination and/or the plan for using the Program's products (i.e. educational materials, assessment instruments, etc.). Tell us, in detail, whether you believe the Program can be replicated elsewhere in your organization and/or in other organizations. Specify organizations that might be appropriate to replicate the Program.

VI. Program Director's Opinion and Reactions

Either in a separate section at the end of the report or integrated into the sections above, please reflect not only on the Program's results but also on the work itself -- the context for the outcomes. While this has been requested in your interim reports, it is particularly important in your final report and you may want to devote more space to this section. **While the objective reporting of your program's accomplishments is important, your interpretation of the experience and insights into the Program's results and possible implications are equally important.**

VII. Report Attachments

Any important documents you want to share with us can be added as attachments. Examples include: consultant reports, abstracts from presentations, educational materials, and charts, tables, graphs or summaries of preliminary data.

FINANCIAL REPORTS

The financial reports should be submitted to the Foundation with the written report. The financial reports include:

> The signed FINAL Grant Financial Report for the entire grant period,
> The Total Program Financial Report for the entire grant period,
> Narrative discussion of Significant Variances and Financial Disclosure, and
> Revised Pro Forma

<u>Format</u>: Excel spreadsheet for the forms are attached.

<u>Narrative Discussions of Significant Deviations and Financial Disclosure</u>: In a short narrative please explain any significant deviations between the approved budget and the reported expenditures. Also, disclose and describe any circumstances in which the Program has benefited financially, including income or cost savings generated by program activities. Describe any other financial support for the Program that has been obtained since the grant was approved.

<u>Budget Deviations and Year End Balances:</u> Although you may over or under spend a line item, you must remain within total approved budget for each grant year unless a revised budget has been submitted and approved. However, the grantee should contact the Foundation about significant line item deviations from the grant budget as far in advance as possible. Balances not expended during the grant year can be carried over into the same line items for the next year with the permission of the Program Officer. **Any significant changes among the line items must be approved <u>before</u> funds are expended.**

Pro Forma for Two Years Following the Grant Period
An updated projected budget and budget narrative for the Program for the two years following the grant period (Pro Forma) must be included in the Final Report. The Pro Forma should include a budget narrative with an explanation for each line item. In general, each narrative statement should include (in as much detail as possible) a description of the specific item, how the specific item relates to the Program, and how you determined the amount shown in your budget arithmetically. The Pro Forma budget must include revenues and expenses based on utilization and program growth assumptions, as well as any capital requirements. If you expect in-kind donations please note them in the budget narrative. Revenues should identify all funding sources and project revenues (3rd party billing, cost savings, philanthropy, etc.).

What you should know: Smart practices

- *Know what's expected:* Ask for grant reporting requirements as soon as you learn that the grant has been approved. Your program officer will appreciate the inquiry, and you'll know from the get-go what you need to produce and when. The majority of funders accept reports in hard copy or by e-mail. There is a trend for those foundations with online grants management software to receive reports directly through the foundation's web site or provider. *Be sure you understand all reporting requirements and that you will be able to submit your report in whatever manner is preferred by the foundation.*

- *Format matters:* While formats will undoubtedly vary, most often, you'll be expected to provide a narrative with basic information about the organization and/or program and what was achieved as a result of the grant, followed by a financial report. Follow the guidelines for reports as you would for proposals: give them what they ask for in the format in which they ask for it. If the basic information they request seems redundant, provide it anyway (in most cases you can lift it directly from the proposal). In special circumstances, a grantee can negotiate to send its own standard report created for other purposes, but that usually depends on the length and nature of the relationship with the funder. An informal survey of funders and a review of grant report forms from across the nation found that the length of reports generally ranged from two to ten pages. In some cases that includes the financial report; in others, a one- to two- page financial report is additional. *The format and length of the report will depend on the funder. More often than not, less is more; review the foundation's web site or ask your foundation contact for guidance.*

- *Deadlines matter:* All grants have a grant period and all reports, be they interim or final, will have a due date. Be sure you understand when and how many reports are due during the grant period. In some cases, a report will be due after the end of the grant period. In others, the report may be due <u>before</u> the end of the period. Always submit a report on time, ideally the week it is due. If for some reason you are unable to meet any deadline, contact the foundation to explain and ask for an extension *The due dates for grant reports and willingness to extend deadlines will depend on the funder; review the foundation's web site or ask your foundation contact for guidance.*

- *Honesty matters:* If goals or objectives were not met, address the issue(s) head on and be clear about why. This is a terrific opportunity to be reflective, to communicate to your funder why things did not go as planned and how you might address the problem moving forward. Candor goes a long way toward building trust with a funder, while omissions (or worse) can create irreparable damage to the funding relationship.

- ***Tell a story:*** In addition to the quantitative aspect, stories infuse humanity into the report and remind the reader that real people are being served, and lives are being changed. It is the human element that engages the reader and reminds him/her about why the project or organization was funded in the first place. *The best reports engage the head and the heart by combining data with stories, case studies, testimonials, etc.*

- ***No need to reinvent the wheel:*** A good grant report can be used in many ways—to set the stage for a request for continued funding, to enhance other agency communications (newsletters, direct mail appeals, web sites, and annual reports), and to capture the good work that's been done along with lessons learned. At the same time, there are sure to be good pieces of writing from various communication vehicles you've already written that can be used in a grant report to minimize the time you need to spend producing your report. Since the successful grant report is the bookend to the successful grant proposal, always revisit your proposal so as to refer back to your original goals and objectives in clear and effective language.

- ***Why bother?*** Contrary to popular belief, grant reports are read, at least by the program officer and/or executive director, and in some cases by the funder's entire board. Foundation staff take cues from all aspects of their interactions with grantees. The ability to submit a complete report on time is part of the assessment process. It communicates your respect for the process and your ability to meet the terms of the grant agreement. *Missed deadlines and incomplete reports bring into question your ability to manage your programs and your organization, and can result in missing grant cycles or not being considered for future funding.*

What you should know: Pet peeves as reported by foundations surveyed

- "Reports that don't answer the questions [in the reporting guidelines]."

- "Padded reports—I'd rather have the relevant information we asked for in fewer pages than fluff to add unnecessary length."

- "Reports that come in with other foundations' names embedded in them. I don't mind if report templates are used for multiple funders, but pay attention to detail. This can be especially embarrassing since my board reads all reports… they feel the grant wasn't appreciated when the report thanks another funder."

- "Grant reports that come in after the deadline without a call or e-mail from the executive director or development officer to give me a heads-up."

- "Missing deadlines as a matter of habit. Once is fine, twice even with a good explanation, but when it's routine, it raises questions."

- "Sending a hard-copy report by overnight mail…what a waste of precious resources!"

- "No communication at all during the grant period until the report shows up—or worse, doesn't show up and I need to contact the organization to remind them the report is due."

- "No mention of major leadership changes in the report, as if it's not important."

Trends in grant reporting

The nature of grant reporting is evolving. Many funders are looking at ways to streamline their processes while ensuring that they get the information they need to assess the efficacy of their investments. New trends being implemented to maximize efficiency include those below.

Common grant report form

There is a trend in the foundation community to streamline processes in an effort to improve foundations' organizational effectiveness, to manage the information and paper overload, and to decrease the amount of time it takes for nonprofits to report on grants. Many foundations are struggling with how to balance their need for accountability and measuring impact with an understanding that grantees should spend their precious time and resources on their meaningful work, not on reports. Among the strategies being implemented is a common grant report (CGR). A CGR is a form that multiple funders agree to accept, usually in the same geographic region. It is made available by individual funders as well as by the regional association of grantmakers to which the funders belong (please see the list at the end of the chapter). In some cases, a funder will accept a CGR, but more detail may also be required or invited. If it is required, be sure you provide it; if a funder invites additional information, do your best to include it. Finally, if your funder does not accept a CGR, you may want to consider using a common grant report form in conjunction with your proposal as a guide for what should go into your report, especially if the foundation has not provided its own form or other guidance.

Reporting and continued support

One welcome trend to the grantee community is having the report serve as part of a request for continued funding. The grant report communicates the successes, challenges, fiscal responsibility, and capacity of the organization to do the work while specific goals and objectives for the coming year are provided in the accompanying cover letter. The due date for a combination report and request for continued funding may differ from the due date for a final report. It is highly unlikely that continued funding will be awarded if the required information is not provided and deadlines are not met, so be sure you're clear on what is required and by what date.

Impact

As discussed elsewhere in this guide, it is critical to think about the impact of your organization's work, how lives were changed and what is different as a result of the grant. The terms may vary, but funders are asking for evidence of *success, results, and/ or outcomes*. Nonprofits must be able to articulate how they define success, the result or impact they are trying to achieve, and the indicators that enable them to know if they have achieved that success or are on the right path. Ideally, you will have provided a "theory of change" in your grant proposal with metrics for short-term and long-term outcomes. Thus, your report would address those as well as unintended outcomes, so that funders will know if and how their support contributed to those results.

Sample grant report

Here is a grant report submitted by On the Move to the S. H. Cowell Foundation for its 2006 support of On the Move's V.O.I.C.E.S. program, the subject of one of the case studies in Chapter 10:

ON THE MOVE

July 12, 2007

Ms. Jamie Allison
Ms. Lise Maisano
S.H. Cowell Foundation
120 Montgomery Street, Suite 2570
San Francisco, CA 94104

Dear Jamie and Lise,

I am writing to report on the activities that have taken place within On The Move's Napa Place-Based Initiative since receiving funding from the S.H. Cowell Foundation in March 2006. As I will describe below, it has been a period of tremendous growth and change. In the period since the original grant was written, the projects described have flourished, while new projects as yet unimagined at the time of Cowell's funding have begun to take shape.

Summary of Activities, Results and Impact
Since March 2006, the following activities have occurred as a result of OTM's efforts across Napa. It is important to note that every activity and initiative described within this report is run by one or more graduates of On The Verge. In total, 15 Vergers are currently hired as OTM staff, including 10 who work in Napa.

On The Verge (*Described in the following three report sections*)
> Group 4: All 11 members graduated in July 2006; five members entered Level 2
> Group 5: Established in February 2006 composed of 13 Napa-based members; all members graduated in February 2007; five members entered Level 2
> Group 6: Established in August 2006, composed of teacher-members from three specific regions, including 4 Napa teachers; all members graduated in June 2007; at least two Napa members intend to enter Level 2

V.O.I.C.E.S. (*Described in the following three report sections*)
> V.O.I.C.E.S. currently serves 150 current and former foster youth between the ages of 16 and 24
> V.O.I.C.E.S. has established individuals programs to address housing, employment, health and wellness, and continuing education.

Napa Educational Equity Initiative (*Described in "Current Napa Developments"*)
> Artlinks arts integration program established at Salvador Elementary in August 2006
> After school programs established at two elementary and one middle school in March 2007
> Leadership academies designed and scheduled to be implemented at one middle and two high schools in August 2007
> Youth councils designed and scheduled to be implemented at three middle high schools in August 2007
> ArtLinks continues and expands to second elementary school in August 2007

The impact of all of these efforts has been tremendous. On the institutional level, agencies across Napa who work in the areas of education, social services, foster youth and community development have come to know On The Move as a valued local asset, capable of high-level

2301 YAJOME STREET, NAPA, CALIFORNIA **94558** • PHONE: **510-599-7785** •
• lmedine@comcast.net • www.onthemovebayarea.org •

collaboration, facilitation of service delivery among unlikely partners, and a dependable agent of change away from "business as usual." Doubt and skepticism has been transformed to interest and respect. As evidenced by the role that V.O.I.C.E.S. youth have been placed in, adult professionals have grown to recognize that young people are not only capable of leading themselves, but that they have critical lessons to provide to the adults themselves. Youth from V.O.I.C.E.S. are continuously in demand to lead workshops and trainings among adult administrators and front line staff at a growing number of Napa youth-serving agencies. Similarly, "Vergers" across Napa are bringing new ways of communicating and doing business to their agencies. In addition, OTM's growing presence within Napa Valley Unified School District – including two elementary, four junior high and two high schools – is demonstrating an expanding range of new a creative options for simultaneously building academic achievement, youth leadership and student voice.

On the individual level, OTM's efforts across Napa have grown to directly impact hundreds of lives and to touch upon thousands. A common element of OTM's work is each individual is impacted differently. OTM's work involves and effects people across at least four generations: children, youth, young adults, and older folks including agency veterans, parents and grandparents. Outcomes on the individual level include increases in elementary test scores; foster youth overcoming long-standing patterns of fear and resistance to become independent adults; young adults stepping into positions of increased responsibility, visibility and salary; community members participating in collaborative planning processes that they had previously believed to be impossible; and veteran agency staff becoming more impactful professionals as a result of training receive from the youth whom they serve.

Services Delivered

Within **On The Verge**, OTM sponsored Groups 4 and 5, composed of 24 Napa-based young professionals, 75% of whom are Latino. All members of both Groups participated in a total of four weekend retreats, as well as 12 months of ongoing coaching and team meetings. Critical themes included:

1. Developing the Personal and Interpersonal/Forming a Team
2. Developing the Interpersonal and Professional/Defining Team's Work
3. Developing the Professional/My Work in the World
4. Performance: Personal, Interpersonal, Professional Integrated in Real Time

Group 5 concluded their year by planning and implementing We Are Here Together: An Intergenerational Dialogue about Leadership and Our Community. On February 16, 2007, On The Move held this symposium, attended by a total of 72 people, including youth and adults ranging in age between 16 and 80; leaders from the non-profit and public sectors; educators; and a diverse mix of ethnic, cultural and economic backgrounds.

In addition to Groups 4 and 5, four Napa teachers have been members of OTV Group 6. In total Group 6 is comprised of 15 experienced educators from Oakland, San Jose and Napa who were convened to design the Reach Institute of School Leadership. Based upon the work of Group 6, the Reach Institute will be pilot this fall, training and credentialing 36 new California teachers.

Within **V.O.I.C.E.S.**, numerous programs and services have developed, built upon a foundation of four core programs: CHOICES, PLACES, SOURCES and CHANGES.

CHOICES – Continuing Post-High School Education Initiative (25 youth served)
Through the CHOICES program, V.O.I.C.E.S. staff and partners encourage and support foster youth through each stage of the higher education experience. This process begins by helping these young adults to think beyond survival and to recognize that college is a genuine option and is critical to future employment. A V.O.I.C.E.S. college counselor is available to help youth apply for scholarships and devise a viable financial plan. Once enrolled, youth continue to receive support, including assistance navigating the community college system and tutoring in a range of subjects.

<u>PLACES – Youth Housing Initiative</u> (21 youth served)
PLACES is a Youth Housing Initiative designed to support emancipated foster youth, ages 18-24, in their transition into self-sufficiency. PLACES participants receive subsidized housing in affordable apartments. PLACES participants receive independent living skills training, college and vocational counseling, personal finance and money management training, job placement support, and ongoing peer and professional support.

<u>SOURCES – Youth Employment Initiative</u> (88 youth served)
V.O.I.C.E.S. employs 18 young people each year between the ages of 16 and 24 at three different levels of work. In addition, V.O.I.C.E.S. partners with local non-profit agencies and with Job Connection, the Napa County job placement agency, to develop a range of training and placement opportunities for up transitional youth.

<u>CHANGES – Access and Support for Health and Wellness</u> (25 youth served)
Struggles with alcohol, drugs, tobacco, gang membership, mental health, physical health and stable relationships are challenges that commonly disrupt the lives of emancipating foster youth as they transition into independence. The CHANGES Program targets youth emancipating from foster care, who are at elevated risk of developing substance abuse problems.

Impact upon Participants
Within both the V.O.I.C.E.S. and On The Verge programs, participants experience a personal evolution, co-create powerful teams, and directly affect the organizations within which they work. At V.O.I.C.E.S., 18 youth have held paid positions as staff, including a youth co-founder who has now become Assistant Director. Participants increasingly witness themselves and their peers taking steps toward independence – as one young person begins paying increasingly large percentages of their own rent for the first time, they watch one friend complete their AA degree, a second friend address alcohol addiction, while a third is employed in their first full-time job. In this way, V.O.I.C.E.S. youth are recognizing their own genuine and previously doubted potential.

Members of On The Verge Group 5 have challenged themselves to initiate change and growth across cultures and generations within their own community. The February 16th symposium served as a culminating performance, demonstrating Group 5's ability to collaboratively plan and implement a very public event, while individually leading the large group process or facilitating small groups of inter-generational and inter-racial community members in real conversations about the leadership and diversity needs of the town.

Changes to the Proposed Project Plan
The proposed project plan outlined a total of seven objectives, listed below. No changes were made to the proposed plan. Over the past year, On The Move and V.O.I.C.E.S. have fully met or exceeded all of the objectives proposed:

	Objective	Status
1.	The V.O.I.C.E.S. Center will be fully operational, serving not less than 100 emancipating and emancipated young people (16-22) in Napa County with services including housing, employment, education, mental health	Exceeded – 150 young people served
2.	OTM will design and document a model for co-located and integrated service delivery for emancipating and emancipated foster youth	Met
3.	Co-located staff from 12 agencies will come together as a fully-functioning team	Exceeded – staff from 20 agencies as a team
4.	V.O.I.C.E.S. partners will clarify, streamline and document the inter-generational, inter-agency decision making process	Met
5.	Directors (top-level decision makers) representing all collaborating agencies will participate as members of the Steering Committee	Met
6.	OTM will launch a second Napa cohort of On The Verge, joining forces with the current group of Vergers for a total of 25 young leaders	Exceeded – 28 Napa Vergers incl. Group 6
7.	VOICES partners, with direction from OTM, will develop a plan for long-term financial sustainability of this initiative	Met

Current Napa Developments

The most recent development in On The Move's Napa place-based efforts is the Educational Equity Initiative. This initiative will touch the lives of over 1,800 youth and adults across Napa, including over 1,000 K-12th grade students across eight public schools. In addition, the Initiative will seek to impact the low levels of civic engagement and academic success among the more than 2,500 Latino students enrolled in the eight partner schools as well as members of their families. The target population for the Napa Educational Equity Initiative are the families of, and individual students who attend McPherson and Salvador Elementary Schools; Creekside, Harvest, Redwood, and Silverado Middle Schools; Napa High School and Valley Oak Continuation High School. All combined, these eight schools enroll a total of 5,555 students, including 2,595 Latino students.

Components Currently Underway

After School Programs: In 2007, OTM began to provide after-school programming at two Napa elementary schools and one middle school. In addition to these three schools, OTM will begin programs at three additional middle schools, bringing the total to six for 2007-08.

ArtLinks: ArtLinks is an academic achievement strategy that pairs art instruction – including music, visual art, theater, and dance – with language arts and mathematics instruction. OTM has partnered with Napa's Salvador Elementary School to co-create ArtLinks, partnering classroom teachers with collaborating artists to re-design curriculum, focusing on the California state standards for education.

Components to Begin in August 2007

Expanding upon these existing efforts, the Napa Educational Equity Initiative will focus on a total of six inter-connected efforts. In combination, these efforts will directly engage and serve at least 1,800 children, youth and adults. These efforts include: Expanded Access to Health and Social Services; Arts Integration for Academic Success; After-School Academic Support; After School Leadership Councils; Youth Leadership Academies; and an Inter-Generational Neighborhood Initiative.

Expanded Access to Health and Social Services: OTM and the McPherson Family Resource Center will facilitate a growing list of partners, including Queen of the Valley Hospital Community Outreach Services, Child Start, the Napa Children's Health Initiative, Clinic Olé and Sister Ann's Dental Clinic in developing new and improved strategies for increasing access to health and social services and engaging low-income families in identify their unmet needs and helping to educate their peers about the resources and services available through the McPherson Family Resource Center.

Arts Integration for Academic Success: In partnership with McPherson and Salvador Elementary Schools, OTM is providing its ArtLinks program to over 630 students, utilizing creative self-expression as a means of bringing meaning and interest to the development of language arts and mathematics proficiency.

After School Leadership Councils: In partnership with Napa Valley Office of Education and Boys & Girls Clubs, OTM will establish and facilitate Youth Leadership Councils at Silverado, Redwood and Harvest Middle Schools. Youth Leadership Council members will learn leadership skills, facilitation skills and evaluation techniques.

Youth Leadership Academies: In partnership with Napa Valley Unified School District, OTM will launch two Youth Leadership Academies – one at Valley Oak Continuation High School and Napa High School and one at Silverado Middle School. Youth will be trained and coached with a cascading leadership model:

> High school and middle school students serve as interns in the McPherson and Salvador Elementary School after school arts programs serving 200 students
>
> High school students work within an intergenerational model with older adults implementing the community project

<u>McPherson Neighborhood Initiative</u>: In conjunction with McPherson Elementary, OTM is exploring partnerships with St. John's Catholic Church, Boys & Girls Club of Napa, and Public Access TV Channels 28 and 29 to engage youth and adults in the McPherson catchment area in intensive community development effort. The ultimate vision for the project is to establish a neighborhood in which parents feel inspired to teach their children what it means to be effective in exercising real choices for themselves, their family and their community and in which McPherson Elementary serves as the hub: A school, park and community center recognized as a safe and welcoming place by both White and Latino families.

Closing – Lessons Learned

Throughout the past year of establishing V.O.I.C.E.S., expanding inter-generational leadership development efforts, and developing the Napa Educational Equity Initiative, key lessons have been learned. At the center is the reaffirmation that when all is said and done, it's all about relationships. In order to do great work in the world, we must be known and know others. Here are some examples of lessons learned:

<u>Community Readiness</u>: Napa is a rural community built upon tradition, long-standing ways of doing business (even in the non-profit sector), and deeply established disparities between the life experiences of Whites and Latinos. OTM had no way to know how community members would respond to a vast set of changes – what we now know is that more than avoiding change, the community has not known how to bring about needed changes, or were less than confident in their ability to enter and affect historically contentious territory. Ultimately, OTM's focus on slowly building and deepening relationships, one person at a time, has helped local agencies become increasingly likely to welcome the changes that are being introduced.

<u>Support for What's "Concrete"</u>: As V.O.I.C.E.S. transitioned from a concept to a fully-functioning program, support for the project expanded quickly. On The Move is composed of visionaries who are comfortable living in the realm of what's possible. V.O.I.C.E.S. has offered the lesson that much of the rest of the world, including community members, agency partners and regional funders, are exponentially more responsive when they have something to get their hands around. The fact that V.O.I.C.E.S. is now a place and a program allows growing numbers of individuals to visit and develop a relationship to this powerful concept put into practice.

<u>Inter-generational Leadership Works</u>: Traditionally, youth and young adults often do not believe that they will treated as valued equals by older adults; similarly, agency veterans and community elders often do not believe that young people are willing to slow down and take in the knowledge and wisdom that comes with age. When members of both groups slow down and enter the learning arena together, as equals, they begin to establish trust and reap the unique insights and teaching of the other. Over time the trust deepens so that not only are members of each group willing to learn from each other, they begin to seek each other out for critical direction and advice.

Thank you for your ongoing support in building inter-generational leadership and youth-led programming across Napa. We look forward to continuing to build our relationship with the S.H. Cowell Foundation.

Sincerely,

Leslie Medine
Executive Director

Conclusion

A grant report provides a systematic and meaningful opportunity for reflection and learning for both the organization and the funder. It promotes communication within the organization and with the funder; it serves as closure for the grant; and quite possibly, it is a bridge to future funding. In order to meet funders' needs, a successful grant report will circle back to the successful proposal. The key is to give the foundation what it asks for when it asks for it and to be able to point to specific examples or indicators of success to which the grant funds contributed.

Resources:

"An Introduction to Grant Reports: Tips and tools for preparing reports for your funders," by Brian Satterfield, TechSoup, May 15, 2007

Forum of Regional Associations of Grantmakers—www.givingforum.org

Colorado Funders Common Grant Report Format/Tips for Users, August 2004 (www.coloradofunders.org)

Common Grant Report Forms are used by member foundations of the following regional associations of foundations:

- Associated Grant Makers (MA)
- Colorado Association of Funders
- Connecticut Council for Philanthropy
- Council of Michigan Foundations
- Council of New Jersey Foundations
- Delaware Valley Grantmakers
- Grantmakers of Western Pennsylvania
- Minnesota Council on Foundations
- Philanthropy New York
- Washington Grantmakers (Washington, D.C.)

Thanks to the following individuals for their responses to my queries:

- Christine Elbel, Fleishhacker Foundation
- Elaine Gold, David B. Gold Foundation
- Mary Gregory, Pacific Foundation Services
- Lise Maisano, S.H. Cowell Foundation
- Elizabeth Share, Wise Giving
- Claire Solot, Marcled Foundation
- Sandra Treacy, W. Clement & Jessie V. Stone Foundation

## 8

The Next Grant

Jane B. O'Connell

Communicate, communicate, communicate

Preparing for the next grant should begin before the ink on the first proposal is dry. Stewardship should be a habit, and a grantee should worry about it all the time. Grantmaking is all about relationships, whether you are looking for a first grant or one after years of repeat grants from the same funder. Whether the funding is from an individual or from a foundation, an ongoing and honest relationship is vital. It is all about trust. And good stewardship is not just making contact with your funder on a regular basis; the potential grantee must work on keeping its house in order and convey information in a timely and appropriate manner. In a difficult economic environment, these relationships are more important than ever. All donors have to make choices and will look for concrete reasons to say "yes" or "no." So it is important to understand what your funder wants. This requires maintaining a strong relationship with the funder and providing information that supports your case.

To shape a relationship with your donors, new or ongoing, involves understanding the motives for philanthropic giving; in fact, institutional funders have the same motivations as individual donors. Joel Fleishman, in his book *The Foundation: A Great American Secret*, discusses motivations for giving: "reasons for making large donations to charitable or other civic organizations vary from the purely altruistic to the self-serving and include a large grey area where the two blend." He goes on to note: "But in the end, it doesn't matter very much. In every sphere of human activity motivations are generally mixed. What does matter, however, is being able to place the results of foundation initiatives side-by-side with what foundations and/or their donors intended to accomplish through their beneficiaries."[1] In essence, the donor and the grantee are both looking for results. The challenge for each entity is to define what are the results of a program, how to measure the outcomes, and most important, what does the information mean in the larger context of the organization's and the funder's goals. Funders are making investments in the organizations they fund. They are stewards of the money and have a moral and legal responsibility to use their resources to the best of their ability and in line with their mission. In many cases they are responsible for carrying out the vision of the founder.

The next few years will be challenging for both nonprofit organizations and the funding community. Getting new grants and maintaining relationships with funders has never been easy, but in recent years grantees and grantmakers have experienced increasing sources of revenues. We are now in a new era of diminished resources, great demand on the providers of services, less government support, and decreased support from individual donors. Technological advances, focus on outcomes, and greater donor sophistication were already changing the approaches to making and seeking grants. Nonprofits will need to become leaner, more strategic, and very nimble. This chapter will look at some of the issues facing nonprofits that want to keep their funders involved, interested, and willing to renew grants. It will also suggest some internal considerations that are becoming more integral to the grantseeking process.

A results-based approach

Recently, there has been a strong trend among funders toward asking nonprofits for outcomes. For many, this is a big shift from earlier attitudes that supported charity or "good works" without much attention to infrastructure or comparative information and data. Today anecdotal evidence may not be adequate. This more rigorous approach is a challenge for both the funders and the grantees, and it requires new ways of thinking about and evaluating an organization's work. Those who are reapplying to a foundation for the same or similar project may become complacent and not worry too much about what they will have to send with a proposal. They most likely are not prepared for a more precise approach or are not sure exactly how to measure or document the results of their programs.

A number of foundations have wrestled with how to change the way they review their grantees' work and have developed matrices and models that achieve their goals. There is no "one size fits all," but both sides of the equation have the goal of improving and maintaining excellent services to their clients. Foundations have designed approaches that fit their cultures. The Altman Foundation struggled with the problem and after much thought worked with the Rensselaerville Institute on a "results-based" process. As Karen Rosa, executive director, explains: "At the core of this approach is a shift from thinking of

---

[1]Fleishman, Joel. *The Foundation: A Great American Secret*. New York: PublicAffairs, 2007, 35.

ourselves only as distributors of resources ('grantmakers') to seeing ourselves as *investors* in what Rensselaerville calls 'creating human gain' for the individuals, families, and communities we serve. And if you think of yourself as an investor, there are three basic questions that you have to answer:

- What do we want to buy? In other words, what are the results that we want to pay for with our grant dollars?

- What are the chances that the nonprofits applying to us will achieve these results, and would these results have been achieved without the work for which the Altman funds are requested?

- Given all the opportunities in front of us, is this the best possible use of our money?

For many this is a significant shift in focus from the old approach of speaking to the values and activities of the organization with a focus on work plans and stories that bring tears to the eye."

The Altman Foundation hopes that this approach will help both staff and board to make better, more informed decisions, and in time, that comparative data will help present a broader picture of the effects of the foundation's grantmaking. In the year that the foundation has been reviewing proposals in the new format, both staff and board find the proposals more informative, interesting, and focused.

Another way to think about a results-based approach is to ask: what do we need to know to improve our work? After all, it is the client, student, or patient who is the ultimate recipient of a grant to an organization. For some nonprofits, looking at outcomes and results will help them manage more strategically and may in time help shape new approaches to their missions. As the nonprofit sector becomes more accustomed to providing data and communicating results, the process could help to identify areas of excellence as well as areas to be strengthened. Internal evaluation is important and often leads to creative thinking; but to change how information is collected and used is not simple and cannot be accomplished instantly. For many agencies, new technology and new data systems have to be installed and staff trained in their use. This transition can be costly and complicated. In the meantime, it is good to remember that a mindset about looking at results can help present a stronger case and possibly improve the service provided. Note also that some types of programs are harder to measure than others. Not all organizations can show that their service produces higher grades on SATs or that more patients are cured with a particular treatment. Creative and thoughtful reports getting at how the agency's mission is carried out will help persuade the funder that the work is important.

Internal matters: Governance and sustainability

Although the focus of a grant proposal is often on a specific program or initiative, and decisions will be made on the merits of the program, increasingly, funders consider governance an important indicator of the strength and sustainability of an organization. For many foundations, in the past governance has not been a focus when reviewing proposals. Recent financial disasters, program failures, and increased government attention have highlighted the fact that some boards have been asleep, too trusting of their management, or unaware of their responsibilities. Even though the Better Business Bureau has published a checklist for many years, the new questions on the 990 forms for 2009 are an indicator of how serious the IRS considers good governance practices.

Boards are the stewards of the nonprofits they lead and are responsible for mission, policy, finances, and appointing the executive director or CEO. This is well described in a recent BoardSource publication on governance, *Advancing Good Governance: How Grantmakers Invest in the Governance of Nonprofit Organizations*: "Good governance—carried out by a strong chief executive in partnership with an engaged strategic thinking board—is the backbone of a healthy and productive nonprofit organization. Like any infrastructure, boards and chief executives require ongoing investment to make sure that their skills are honed, relationships are nurtured, and new challenges are met."[2] In addition, real board leadership requires more than just reading balance sheets and raising money. In another important book on governance, *Governance as Leadership: Reframing the Work of Nonprofit Boards*, the authors point out, "As responsible fiduciaries, trustees endeavor to conserve and enhance an organization's tangible assets like finances, facilities, endowment and personnel. In the strategic mode, boards attempt to convert these same assets, as well as intangibles like organizational traditions, ethos, and image into comparative advantage."[3]

Organizations led by strong executive directors and creative boards will have more credibility with funders. Dynamic leadership is the key to a strong organization. Funders, rightfully concerned about succession, will sometimes wait until new leadership is in place to renew funds for a program. Often, boards and management of a strong organization underestimate the importance of sharing details of succession planning with their funders. Sustainability is not just a financial concern, it is a leadership and management issue.

Many organizations are simply too busy and understaffed to focus on how to reinvent themselves and to think about modern ways to approach their work. There are a number of available resources to help guide a nonprofit in assessing its health

---

[2]Hedge, Kathy K., Eva Nico, and Lindsay Fox. *Advancing Good Governance: How Grantmakers Invest in the Governance of Nonprofit Organizations*. *BoardSource*. March 2009. (www.boardsource.org/UserFiles/File/pdf/AdvancingGoodGovernance.pdf).

[3]Chait, Richard P., William P. Ryan, and Barbara E. Taylor. *Governance as Leadership: Reframing the Work of Nonprofit Boards*. Hoboken, NJ: John Wiley & Sons, Inc., 2005, p. 161.

and evaluating performance. These topics can be excellent discussion items for board and staff retreats or agenda items at board meetings. There are many good consultants and a number of nonprofit organizations that will provide assistance in the management and program areas that an organization needs. There are funders who will make grants or provide programs to help nonprofits build their capacity. Governance is a board's primary responsibility, and if a board does not appear to be aware of this mandate, it behooves senior management of the organization to bring the issues to the board. Often, development officers do not consider governance to be part of their responsibility. But unless their organization is well governed, it is hard to present a full picture for a potential funder.

Stewardship—Your funder as your friend

Let's say that you have your house in order, and you now want to work on your relationships with your funders. The reason a funder found your organization worthy of a grant in the first place is often a good indicator of willingness to renew your funding, but this is not necessarily always the case. Do not relax or become complacent. Funders have policies about renewals and how many renewals they will consider. In a more competitive financial environment, they are tightening their requirements and taking new approaches. They should not be taken for granted and may be looking more intensely at some of the areas that are indicators of the strength of the nonprofit. Among them are:

- *Mission and vision*—Has the board and staff reviewed the core values as stated in the organization's mission? Has there been "mission creep"?

- *Program effectiveness*—Obviously it is the program, or, in the case of general operating support, the mission, that is the reason to make a grant. Has there been an evaluation of the program? Are there performance measures? Is the leadership reviewing data and outcomes?

- *Planning*—Is there a strong planning process both on the program side and in the financial area? Does the organization have a multi-year plan, and is it reviewed frequently? Is there a financial plan that includes a multi-year fundraising strategy? Is there a contingency plan?

- *Finances*—Does the organization have its financial house in order? Do the board and finance committees review the financials on a timely basis? Financial health has become a major focus as foundations review proposals, and sustainability is a deep concern. Are there plans for reducing budgets and perhaps service in tough economic times?

- *Governance*—Is the organization's governance structure in order? Are policies and procedures in place and reviewed regularly? Is the board taking responsibility for governance seriously?

- *Sustainability*—Are there contingency plans for possible changes in leadership and/or senior management?

In preparation for this chapter, I asked several of my colleagues for their thoughts on good stewardship. Of all the ideas, opinions, and suggestions there was one theme—*communicate*. You are trying to build a culture of trust with your funder. Many funders consider themselves partners in your mission and want to know how the project and the organization are doing. As you plan how you will relate to your funder, consider some of these questions:

- Did you establish a strong relationship in the beginning? If you did, then it is easier to continue. Don't wait until the next proposal is due.

- Has the original contact with the funder changed, and, as a result, was there a period of time when there were gaps in contact with a funder? All is not lost; you can and should start immediately.

- Have there been some concerns over program results, financial issues, or leadership? These need to be addressed promptly, carefully, and directly.

- Have you reported on the ongoing grant on time and properly? If not, be humble, then make contact and apologize.

- If your organization has been "on hiatus" for a time because the foundation has a policy of taking a break, have you been communicating with the foundation in the interim? Many foundations appreciate a periodic update.

- Do you still fit the foundation's guidelines? It may happen that the donor's priorities no longer fit a nonprofit's mission. Don't try to force a fit, but have a conversation with your contact.

Make your funders feel special

There are the traditional activities that a good organization has in its public relations arsenal, such as publications, web sites, events, and e-mail blasts. These are important and the frequency, appropriateness, and impact should be examined on a regular basis. The trend to a more web-based public relations approach is important, but do not give up all the old ways of communicating too quickly. Standard approaches, however, are not the only way you would talk to a close friend. Do treat your funders as close friends (they are) and seize on moments when a more personal contact is appropriate, when it provides a chance to tell your story. The funder should feel special. Here are some actual examples, provided by two foundation program officers:

- One group provides year-round opportunities to "look under the hood" of its education programs while they are still works in progress. They send out frequent invitations, but leave it up to you to respond, so that it does not feel heavy-handed. There are usually enough options so that one can fit your schedule. While we fund specific programs, the organization extends invitations to others we do not fund and encourages donors to explore the breadth of what they do.

- Prior to a grant anniversary, a nonprofit initiated a discussion of its strategic plan and asked to postpone coming back to us for funding since it was fleshing out a strategy for increasing access to high-quality educational experiences. The nonprofit was candid also about the fact that its afterschool program was not capable of making up for what students were missing by attending underperforming public schools, particularly the older students who are less likely to attend after school programs regularly. The nonprofit's candor made me more receptive to considering funding their school support program when the opportunity came up later on. Often organizations talk about their relationships with parents; during my site visit last fall, this nonprofit arranged for me to speak with parents at multiple stages of the program.

- A performing arts youth development program, which had undergone a somewhat difficult executive transition, handled the introduction of the new executive director to the funding community very well. Partly because of the leadership transition, the organization had a very tough year financially and appeared to be vulnerable. Once in place, the new executive director visited with each funder and explained her vision for the organization and her board development strategy. In addition, about six months into her tenure, the organization held a funders' briefing for current supporters as well as future prospects. A number of board members participated in the briefing, which included a financial overview and a development plan going forward. In addition, a few board members talked about why they joined the organization and how the new executive director's leadership had re-energized the board. Overall, you got a strong sense of the organization's commitment and engagement. The briefing was one of the best I've been to because it highlighted the programmatic strengths of the organization, while also addressing issues of governance and sustainability.

- A new initiative designed to help build the geriatric care workforce was data-driven from the start and used the information gathered about participants and initial results to engage with funders a few times a year. The organization organized webinars and invited all funders to review their findings to date as a group and to offer suggestions about how to address issues raised by the data. The briefings generally occurred between grant requests and were mutually beneficial to both the funders and the grantee. They gave funders a sense of how a new, and therefore risky, initiative was unfolding so that there were no major surprises at reporting time. In addition, the briefings gave the grantee the opportunity to use its funders as a resource to address challenges. For example, in areas where the program was weak, we were able to suggest partnerships the organization could pursue to strengthen its services to participants and, hence, improve results.

What if the news is less than favorable?

Sometimes there is a temptation not to report bad news. In a crisis situation, one of the first calls should be made to your funders. Every organization will have a period of crisis or change. Be thoughtful about how and how much you communicate about your problems. The approach should depend on your relationship with your funders and their operating style. On the other hand, do not forget to celebrate good news with your funder.

If there is a scandal or for some reason you will be on the front page of the *New York Times* (or worse, the nightly news on television), forewarn your funders. No one likes to be blindsided. If there are significant financial changes either in the total budget or in the specific program being funded, funders care. In difficult financial times, do communicate any major changes in your overall financial stability and any significant budget changes.

If there are changes in leadership or project personnel, those who are investing in you should know as soon as possible and not when the renewal letter goes out. Leadership is vital to the success and effectiveness of an organization's operations and can be one of the most important factors in a foundation's decision to invest. It does not hurt to inform your funders about the search process and the timing, and this should include senior staff such as the program or development officer who is involved in a funded program. Communicating this way will help to allay fears of confusion and disruption in the organization. When a new leader is appointed, try to arrange for an opportunity for your funder to meet the person either one-on-one or at a reception.

If the funded program design or scope changes, let the funder know sooner rather than later. This can provide a good opportunity to have a conversation with your program officer and highlight some new data or assessments of the programs (even if the grant period is not complete), as well as to have a preliminary conversation about future funding. It is even appropriate in some instances to discuss other funding opportunities with a funder. Sometimes a funder will recommend a grantee to a peer. But keep in mind that you may be putting your funding contact on the line if you request such a referral, and some cannot take on such a proactive role.

Often at the time of a site visit or a meeting, several officers of your organization are present. It is not unusual to hear different stories from program staff, development officers, financial officers, executive directors, and even board members. It is important that these different perspectives are aligned and that clarity of purpose is communicated. The program staff usually determines the objectives and outcomes of the programs. The development office is not as involved in program design or implementation, and those individuals may not communicate about the program with similar emphasis. Everyone involved should be on the same page.

Your funder as your advocate

Believe it or not, foundation staff members are your advocates. They represent your organization at staff meetings and in the board room, and they often make your case. Share your successes (and failures) with them. They take great personal interest in the organizations in their portfolio. Try to understand their priorities and how you fit. Visit web sites and read annual reports and articles in the press for changes and developments at a foundation. In his book, *Yours for the Asking*, Reynold Levy, the president of Lincoln Center, a master fundraiser, and someone who is not always an admirer of foundation procedures, points out:

> Learning what your opposite number values in a nonprofit's proposal and performance will help you to prepare a solicitation custom made for that foundation. Stay determined. Do not underestimate how much merit matters. On the other side of the table are generally people of intelligence and goodwill, trying to dispense philanthropy in the most advantageous way with the highest impact on the problem being addressed.[4]

A foundation has a constituency, and its representatives want to communicate the value of their work. Share your information, news stories, awards, and profiles of your staff and volunteers. Funders may even use your stories in their own communications or in their presentations to their boards. Grantmakers do like to be invited to events that show off programs. But do not be disappointed if they decline. They can't possibly accept all the invitations they get; the invitation itself is a form of stewardship.

While some funders have a hands-off approach to their grantees, even they expect to hear if there are critical issues emerging in your organization. Each foundation is different, and there are those who do not want much dialogue between grants. So it is important to ascertain what they do require. No matter how engaged a foundation wants to be, or not, there are a number of no-nonsense rules that will help establish a good relationship; although they may seem obvious, some of the following do not always happen, and when they don't, in many funders' minds this is unforgivable:

- Send timely and almost immediate acknowledgement letters. If for some reason formal acknowledgements take some time, a short, personal note goes a long way. In addition, it does not hurt to make a phone call when the grant is received.

- Follow reporting requirements.

- Meet the deadlines for both reports and new proposals.

One executive director of a foundation remarked: "We don't ask much from grantees, especially between grants; so when they fail to report when they should, that is a huge black mark against them that may take several years for them to erase. So, to

---

[4]Levy, Reynold. *Yours for the Asking: An Indispensable Guide to Fundraising and Management*. Hoboken, NJ: John Wiley & Sons, Inc., 2008, p. 83.

summarize, we don't require anything from grantees between grants and we don't even expect much during the grant. But if they can't do what we ask at the start and finish of the grant, them we are not likely to make another grant to them." These are harsh words, but not unreasonable.

An organization may make an excellent case for re-funding, but even with the best of relationships and perfect stewardship, your proposal may be declined. Reynold Levy notes: "If you formally apply and are turned down, did you endeavor to find out the whys and wherefores, not in order to lodge a protest but to learn how to improve?"[5] A declination does not mean you should not continue to cultivate and maintain a relationship with the funder, unless it is clear that your organization no longer fits within the guidelines of the foundation. Even then, treat the foundation as a friend. After all, it has supported you and considers you part of the family. Foundations are often understaffed and cannot return your calls or e-mails immediately. Don't be a pest, but do be persistent—a hard balance to maintain. There may be other opportunities in the future.

The future: Opportunities and challenges

Beginning with September 11th, the 21st century has been a period of great instability. History may show that for the nonprofit sector the most unsettling changes began in 2007 with the indicators of an economic downturn. In 2008, the financial support of nonprofits seriously declined. *Giving USA 2009: The Annual Report on Philanthropy for the Year 2008* notes that all sectors are down except religion and public benefit works. Many foundations have lost value in their assets. Even if the economy improves soon, foundations will not be increasing their giving. Most work on a three-year averaging formula and may not have increased assets until 2011 at the earliest. Fortunately there are a few who have more available assets, and some boards are authorizing grants at the same level as they have in the past. However, securing renewal funding will be more competitive. Even if a nonprofit has been funded in the past and has "communicated" with energy and thoughtfulness, getting the next grant will be more challenging.

Crises are not all bad. The economic realities will force many nonprofits to reexamine their missions and operations; foundations will become more strategic in their giving policies and when better times come again, and they will, many nonprofits will emerge stronger and with a renewed sense of purpose. We all know that the demand for services will not diminish. It is more important than ever for funders and grantees to dialogue with each other. The work of the nonprofit sector is a vital component in the lives of millions. Grantmakers and grantees have the same goal—to make the world a better place for all who use the services provided. It is, in the end, all about trust.

---

[5]Levy, p. 82.

9

The Grantmaker/Grantee Partnership

Michael Seltzer

Unmet expectations

According to the reputed memoirs of the grants manager for King Ferdinand and Queen Isabella of Spain, Christopher Columbus' record as a grantee was a complete washout. In his proposal, he had promised to find a new route to the East Indies and Asia, accessing the lucrative silk, spices, and opiates trade for the benefit of his donor. Sadly, our fearless navigator had severely underestimated the circumference of the earth and the distance across the Atlantic to the Indies. Instead, he found a series of inhospitable islands more than eight thousand miles away from his real destination, and to make matters worse, his crew members brought new contagious illnesses back from their journeys. Many of them subsequently joined the army of King Charles VIII in his invasion of Italy in 1495, resulting in the spread of disease across Europe and as many as five million deaths. Christopher Columbus' funder eventually threw him in prison in 1500.

Talk about unintended consequences of a grant!

Fortunately, more than five hundred years later, grantees no longer face imprisonment for failure to accomplish everything they had promised to do as part of a grant proposal. But they do face the possibility of "non-renewal" if they do not render positive results to their funder. How can today's Christopher Columbus, who is prepared to sail into the uncharted waters of social change or some other worthwhile endeavor, deliver on his promises to his organization's donor?

In the best-case scenario the grantee is able to go full speed ahead in carrying out the set of activities described in the original proposal and to report back to the funder as scheduled regarding the accomplishments and positive outcomes of the grant. Both parties are satisfied and become excited about their future partnership. The stage is then set for discussion of a possible renewal grant.

What do we mean by a "partnership" between funder and grantee? For the grantee this means being sensitive not only to your own organization's interests but to the interests of the funder as well. You will want to do everything you can to ensure that your project will help fulfill the foundation's philanthropic mission and contribute to its success as an effective grantmaker. For the funder, being a full partner with a grantee means confidence in the leadership and pride in the affiliation with the particular organization, and most of all a complete sense of confidence that the grantee can be relied upon to do what it said it would do while adhering to today's best practices.

Much can and often does occur to derail this optimal scenario. Here are a few examples of things that can go wrong:

- A project director at a prominent university neglects to ascertain that his institution has submitted the signed grant agreement letter to the funder. He discovers this oversight two years after he has completed the funded project. He calls his foundation program officer apologetically to request that the grant dollars be released, even though the university had already paid all of the project expenses out of its own coffers, thus strongly suggesting that the grant was not really needed.

- A foundation executive learns from a news article that an employee of one of its grantee organizations has embezzled funds from the organization. While somewhat sympathetic, she is quite miffed that the grantee did not extend her the courtesy of contacting her right away, and not even after the news article appeared. Mostly, however, she is eager to hear what specific corrective steps the grantee is planning to take to address the situation—both the missing funds and the bad publicity.

- A grantee submits a request for renewal funding even before his organization has submitted a report on the outcomes of the initial grant.

- The executive director of a grantee organization resigns mid-grant, but no one at the organization thinks to send a letter to supporters explaining why the director left and what the organization is doing to assure continuity while it looks for a replacement CEO.

- A foundation changes its program priorities and/or grantmaking strategies after awarding a substantial grant to an organization and fails to notify its executive director. As a result the grantee organization that no longer "fits" the funder's guidelines has little time to find replacement funding and less than a year later is forced to shut down.

- A foundation abruptly chooses to exit a field of endeavor where it has been active for many years. The funder offers no assistance to its current grantees, such as transitional support or introductions to other funders.

In some of these real-life scenarios, there is evidence of carelessness or lack of common sense on the parts of both grantee and grantmaker. By far the biggest problem, however, is a relationship hampered by a lack of communication and, in some cases, trust. How can a grant recipient deliver on the promissory note to the donor that a grant award represents? What are the most important outcomes that the grantee should focus on to sustain what will hopefully be an ongoing successful partnership between both parties? To what extent is the grantee's success a responsibility shared by both the donor and the recipient?

Understanding your grantmaker

There are some 100,000 grantmakers in the United States and growing numbers of institutional donors around the globe. They include independent, family, corporate, community, and other public foundations and similar charitable bodies worldwide. The sheer scope and breadth of the philanthropic sector makes it difficult to make too many generalizations about *all* foundations and their respective policies. We can, nonetheless, provide some general precepts aimed at bridging the perennial gap between those on either side of the grantmaking equation.

It is easy for the grantor/grantee relationship to go awry if there is not a clear, shared understanding up front of what the grant recipient is expected to accomplish during the actual grant period. In many cases, as is all too familiar for those seeking funding for their organizations, grantmakers do not provide sufficient information to the public on their programmatic interests. In 2007, only 10.2 % of the nation's private foundations reported publishing an annual report, and as of 2009 only about 4,000 foundations have web sites. Annual reports and web sites, however, generally do not shed much light on a foundation's intellectual and analytical decision-making framework, theories of change, strategies, and so on. There are exceptions, of course. For example, the Ford Foundation has added information about its grantmaking strategies in its 13 fields of interest to its web site. This information is useful both to those seeking support from the foundation and to Ford's recent grantees.

It may actually be the case that a foundation and its grantee have widely disparate notions of what each hopes to see happen over the duration of the grant. Even though the original grant proposal stands as a point of reference and the grant letter as a form of contract, there may nonetheless be a raft of unspoken assumptions on the part of either or both parties to the grant. For this reason it is important for the grantee to glean as much information as possible before the actual grant commences and for direct and effective communication to take place as often as necessary during the course of the grant period.

Beyond what you already know from studying your funder when it was only a prospect, and what you learn when you read the grant award letter very carefully, the wise grantee would be well advised to determine as much as possible about the programmatic priorities and strategies of a new foundation donor. For those foundations that have web sites and those that issue newsletters, annual reports, or other printed materials, this type of information is not difficult to ascertain. It may be possible also to query other organizations that have successfully secured more than one grant from the funder about expectations, operating procedures, what to look out for, how best to cement the relationship, and so on. You'd be surprised how generous those who work for your colleague organizations will be with this type of insider information.

Seeking clarification of expectations

Most importantly, if you are able to meet (in person or by phone) with a program officer or other funding representative either during the proposal review process or immediately after the grant has been awarded, this represents a fortuitous opportunity to ask the right questions. Once you've already received the grant, you no longer need to "sell" the funder on the benefits of your organization and its program. Now is the time to ask targeted questions of your program officer to fill in gaps in your own knowledge about the funder and to set your organization on the right path to a successful and productive relationship with your grantmaker. Here are important pieces of information you will want to try to glean from this conversation:

Are there desired outcomes on the part of the funder, beyond what is in the grant proposal or award letter? Examples might include, actual documented and measurable changes in a set of social or economic conditions and/or policies; growth in size, scope, or capacity of your organization; indications of positive change or advancement in a larger field of endeavor; the development of present and future leadership.

Are there specific assessment methods your funder expects you to adopt? This is critical to ask about, if your proposal included no specific plan to evaluate the success of your grant project. Some foundations prescribe a "theory of change" or "logic model" that they expect their prospective applicants to submit as part of their grant award letter. Others may include a section about these types of items as part of their grant reporting form. While some funders may prefer quantifiable success indicators, others may enjoy anecdotal or qualitative evidence of an organization's effectiveness. If it's not obvious, be sure to ask about this.

What will your relationship with the funder be like once the grant is awarded? How often will you have contact with the funding representative, and what form is that contact likely to take? With the many options available today, it is important to determine what is your program officer's preferred method of communication. Are there others at the foundation or even other grantees that the funder would like you to be sure to keep abreast of your progress?

If the opportunity arises for recognition of the grant in the form of a press release, mention in the media, or public acknowledgement at an event, what form should that recognition take? Keep in mind that some funders shun the spotlight, while others expect to get public credit in return for their philanthropic activities.

What about the possibility of future funding? If (and only if) it seems appropriate, even at the outset of the grant, you may want to inquire about the possibility of additional funding when the grant period ends. You should ask when it would be best to initiate discussions in regard to the possibility of a renewal grant. Today's foundation program officers generally understand that dramatic changes, such as stemming the tide of global warming or providing urban youth with quality public education or reducing violence against women, are rarely achievable in the average grant period, whether that is one or two or three years. They hope that during the actual grant period, your organization's leadership will be able to demonstrate the efficacy of a particular methodology or strategy and evidence of promising practices that others can learn from to inform their work. At the same time they realize that a goodly portion of a nonprofit executive's time is spent drumming up the dollars needed to continue the organization's important work. So it is not out of line to inquire about whether or not this is likely to be a one-time grant.

What might the funder have to offer its grantees beyond the provision of grant dollars? Most foundation program officers make themselves available to their grantees to provide advice during the course of the grant and will want to know of any major changes that occur. But some foundations provide services that go well beyond the typical grantee/grantmaker relationship. Some give additional "in-kind" support, such as technical assistance, expert one-on-one consultation, use of meeting and exhibition facilities, access to opinion leaders, networking opportunities, and general financial, management, and communications know-how. You as a new grantee will want to take advantage of all services available to you.

Here are some examples of foundations that go beyond the simple awarding of grants:

• Strengthening Grantee Capacity

  The Robert Wood Johnson Foundation of Princeton, New Jersey, has long invested in building its grantees' capacity to communicate with one another and the larger public through annual meetings, technical assistance workshops on communications strategies and tactics, and the creation of an extranet site to offer research and convening resources to grantees.

The W.K. Kellogg Foundation of Battle Creek, Michigan, in conjunction with the Fieldstone Alliance, designed and makes available an Action Lab to its grantees. The Action Lab provided a range of capacity-building resources in an interactive format, including one-on-one expert consultation for those who were eligible.

• Helping Grantees Access Donated Meeting or Exhibition Space

The Bauman Family Foundation of Washington, D.C. offers its conference space for grantee activities and convenes program meetings to which grantees are invited. The Daniels Fund makes its Denver, Colorado, meeting spaces available free of charge to nonprofits serving Colorado, Wyoming, New Mexico, or Utah. The Meadows Foundation of Dallas, Texas, owns and operates the 22-acre Wilson Historic District, a nonprofit office park that preserves Dallas' Victorian structures and encourages the nonprofit community to work collaboratively in rent-free space.

• Connecting You to Other Resources

The James Irvine Foundation of San Francisco, California, offers a list of tools and resources (including publications, professional organizations, and online materials) at its web site to help grantees and other nonprofits (including foundations) increase their effectiveness.

• Introducing Grantees' Work to Key Opinion Makers

A number of foundations are taking active steps to introduce key opinion leaders in their fields of endeavor to the work of their "partner" organizations. The Eugene and Agnes Meyer Foundation of Washington, D.C., and The Sister Fund in New York City have redesigned their annual reports to draw more attention to the work of the organizations that they support.

The road to success

So far we've explored what can go wrong in a grantee/grantmaker relationship when both parties do not tend it properly, we've posited a series of questions that the grantee should ask to ensure that everything related to its stewardship of a foundation's grant money stays on track, and we've looked at the many ways grantmakers can and do assist those grantees who seek their help. The reality is that not every grantmaker/grantee interaction progresses smoothly, and for most there are at least a few bumps in the road. Yet much can be done to transform the character of the relationship to ensure the outcomes that both parties desire.

Meanwhile, the standard roles played by both parties may in fact be undergoing transformation. While the unequal balance of power between donor and recipient may persist, despite concrete efforts aimed at "leveling the playing field," a growing body of evidence now exists that the actual character of the relationship is slowly beginning to shift. No longer is the transaction simply financial and vertical in nature. A number of forward-thinking foundations and corporate grantmakers are playing a role akin to that of an ongoing investor. They are sharing responsibility for their grantee partners' successes and failures. Similarly, nonprofits are taking parallel steps to increase their own effectiveness and to communicate more openly with their donors. Much, of course, remains to be done.

Changing technology has created a new electronic tool kit for both parties to take advantage of as they seek to build stronger relationships and maximize results. Communications are now global and instantaneous, and happen around the clock, while the capabilities of the web have created an expectation of openness, sharing, and participation. Indeed, pervasive bloggers are publicly scrutinizing everything imaginable and forcing doors open. Philanthropy has not escaped bloggers' attention, as is testified to by the multiplying blogs related to our field. The social, networked nature of the web has resulted in a shift in how we communicate, giving us the tools for two-way dialogue instead of one-way broadcasting, allowing organizations to build stronger relationships with all of their stakeholders, hopefully with donors and grantees being near the top of each other's list.

These are healthy trends for many reasons. Both parties can become more accessible and transparent as institutions. Relationships are likely to become stronger, more interactive, and more immediate. And when such relationships thrive, there is a greater likelihood of a better return on the grant dollar for both parties. Finally, external demands for greater accountability and overall transparency of all institutions in the private, public, and charitable sectors bode well for enhanced relationships between funders and recipients.

Since we've acknowledged that this relationship is a two-way street, what follows are check-lists of responsibilities for both parties to a grant.

Grantee's responsibilities

Upon receipt of funding

- Promptly send a thank-you letter.
- Inquire if the funder has any restrictions or preferences regarding public mention of the grant award (if not indicated in the grant agreement letter).

- Return a signed copy of the grant agreement letter, and keep a copy for your files.

- Schedule a meeting to clarify which outcomes are most important to the funder and to solicit any suggestions that your program officer might have.

- Offer your program officer the opportunity for a site visit, or more than one.

Documenting activities and outcomes

- Share important news with your funder as you proceed with implementation, including "bad" news and lessons learned.

- Review evaluation or self-assessment protocol to ensure that it still is appropriate and discuss any possible changes with the funder.

- Report on grant outcomes fully and on schedule.

- Keep track of any contacts with your funder.

Being a good philanthropic citizen

- Take advantage of opportunities for networking, peer learning, and technical assistance, especially those provided by your funder.

- Provide occasional opportunities for corporate and foundation staff to participate in the life of your organization.

- Recognize foundation and corporate supporters in appropriate ways in organizational literature and at events.

- Reach out to key relevant opinion leaders and subject experts to inform them of your work.

Funder's responsibilities

Funders should also be cognizant of certain best practices to engage in with their grantees once a grant has been awarded. Here is a brief checklist:

Being transparent and accessible

- Clarify expectations up front.

- Be available to lend an ear and a hand, if needed.

- Encourage and model a culture of candor.

- Check in on your grantees' progress periodically.

- Alert grantees to any changes in program priorities that might affect your foundation's ongoing support of their work.

Making available non-cash resources as well as reputational assets

- Offer to make introductions to other donors, journalists, and key opinion makers.

- Promote the work of grantees at your own web site, annual report, and elsewhere.

Building mutually supportive relationships

- Encourage horizontal and vertical communications.

- Solicit feedback from grantees and act on it.

- Inform your grantees about grant renewal procedures, and do this early on in the relationship.

- Share lessons learned and work toward a culture of learning.

And what if we "fail"?

To paraphrase Paul Ylvisaker, a beloved foundation mentor and legendary public affairs director of the Ford Foundation, foundations provide the funds to create society's passing lane on the social change highway. That road, however, has many forks and off-ramps, and the skillful nonprofit leader may have to travel along several routes before she or he reaches the desired destination. Some foundation officials with an appetite for risk understand that even taking a wrong turn can produce much-needed knowledge of value to the larger field of endeavor. After all, while Christopher Columbus did not find the speedier route to the Indies, he did discover the "new world." Perhaps a wiser Queen Isabella would have realized that he had produced something of greater value than what he had originally set out to do.

A few brave foundations have sought to sanction high-risk grantmaking by going so far as to publicize their "failures." Yet those funders are still few and far between. For the nonprofit grantee, it is important to gauge in advance which outcomes your particular funder is most interested in, and to be sure to document those you achieve. The results will please you both. The rule of thumb for both nonprofit and foundation leaders today is to seek out new ways to build a relationship based on transparency and trust. At the beginning and the end of the day, both parties are interested in the same outcome: stronger organizations that can successfully advance their respective missions.

## 10

The Successful Grant: Case Studies

Elan DiMaio

Introduction

In the course of preparing materials for this guide, we interviewed a group of foundation representatives and nonprofit grantees who volunteered to participate in the *After the Grant* project. We asked them a series of questions about their own experiences with the grantmaker/grantee relationship. By far the most important question we posed was: What makes a grant successful? We also canvassed our friends and colleagues in the philanthropic community, asking them to nominate specific successful grant projects that would serve as models for others to emulate.

In this final chapter of the guide we will address the issue of what makes a grant successful by means of three case studies culled from the various grant projects recommended to us. Experience has shown that novice grantees learn best from others' success. There's nothing like actual examples of things that really worked to spur people on to set high performance standards themselves. Our focus in identifying grants for the case studies was on those that actually played out well in terms of shared expectations, useful communication, and outcomes that were demonstrably excellent, in some cases far exceeding expectations.

We selected the three case studies you will find in this chapter primarily because in each case both grantmaker and grantee had words of high praise for the manner in which they unfolded and the results achieved. In each instance the grantee managed the program well and exhibited many facets of sound stewardship of the grantmaker's funds. In each instance, as well, the foundation program officer assigned to the grant proved to be accessible, communicative, and committed to ensuring a positive outcome. We chose grantmakers of different sizes and types. (One is a community foundation; one is a small family foundation; and one is a large foundation that funds internationally.) We looked for funders based in different geographic areas (Georgia, California, and Michigan), and we sought out grant projects of different sizes and scope, benefiting different kinds of audiences. Despite all of that variety, in reading these cases studies you will note that these three successful grants have a great deal in common. What follows as a prelude to the cases is an attempt to tease out some of those similarities.

What do successful grant projects have in common?

Based on this admittedly tiny sample, it is evident (and indeed no surprise) that a good deal of what is deemed successful derives from the relationship between the foundation program officer and the nonprofit staff member tasked with carrying out the grant project. In each of our case studies these relationships have gone on for some time (the most recent having begun in 2004), and even when the nonprofit representative was not an actual grantee, she was familiar with the funder in various other capacities. But what speaks even more to the success of this relationship is that in all three cases foundation support is ongoing and/or future funding forthcoming. For the novice grantee, this is an excellent goal to shoot for: a funder who values your organization's work to such an extent that he or she wants to continue to support it, even if for a different project entirely.

The second aspect that stands out as a commonality among all three cases is the high degree of honest and frequent communication that took place between the program officer and the grantee. In two of the three cases substantial discussions took place before a proposal was even submitted, and in at least one instance, the funder admits to having helped shaped the proposal to ensure that it met the mutual goals of each organization. Site visits were conducted in all three instances, but at different times during the proposal review and award cycle. Communication between funder and grantee took a variety of forms, ranging from casual conversation when they happened to run into one another, to phone calls when an issue came up that needed clarification, to e-mails, to invitations to events, to the formal site visits already mentioned. All six individuals we interviewed for the case studies basically expressed the same critical piece of advice: It is important to share both good and bad news with your funder, and to do it as soon as something newsworthy occurs. Word travels fast in philanthropic circles, and it is universally viewed as a negative if a funder hears of any significant news about a grantee organization from someone other than that grantee.

The third thing that all three grantee organizations, highlighted in our case studies, have in common is strong financial management systems already in place prior to receiving the grant. This, of course, is a core aspect of good stewardship of someone else's money. Each funder expressed admiration for the way grant funds were handled, allocated, and reported back on, in line with the initial proposal budget. That's not to say that changes didn't occur during the course of the grant period. When they did occur, however, good communication practices were adopted, and the nonprofit staffer made sure to confer with the foundation program officer for advice on what adjustments would be permissible. One common element of sound financial management at each organization was consistency, in that one individual was assigned to follow through on all aspects related to the grant.

The next item all three had in common was excellence in reporting back on use of grant funds. Only one of the three grants covered in our case studies was complex enough to require a formal external evaluation, but all three nonprofit organizations submitted final (and in two of the three cases interim) grant reports that included careful and thoughtful assessment of outcomes vis-à-vis the objectives for the grant. (See Chapter 7 for one such final grant report.) The very common sense answer we often received when we asked what made these particular grants stand out was that the nonprofit did what it had said it would do, spending the grant money accordingly, and meeting its deadline. It sounds very simple, but indeed is the essence of good stewardship.

Remaining common threads we can point to among all three cases are more ephemeral and difficult to pin down. Several spoke of the sense of a "common fit" between the missions of the two organizations, grantmaker and grantee. All three nonprofit managers expressed great appreciation for their funders, and vice versa. Normal courtesy seemed to go a long way in cementing these relationships. More often than not the nonprofit grantee deferred to the funder's wishes, (having already asked about them), as to what form communication should take, how frequently it should occur, and what formats to adopt in reporting. While on the one hand the grantees seem to have taken pains to confer with their funders when difficult issues arose or hard decisions needed to be made, the funders were quick to point out that it's a two-way street. Nonprofit grantees often have expertise in a particular subject field and experience with certain audiences well beyond the knowledge base or skill set of foundation program officers. In at least one instance the grantmaker owned up to having gone to the grantee for advice about a particular topic, unrelated to the grant. Basic suggestions like being sure to invite your funder to relevant events kept coming up. Even if the program officer was unable to attend, simply receiving the invitation seemed to go a long way toward making him or her feel valued and "in the loop" in terms of what was going on at the grantee organization.

Methodology

Once we had identified the three grants we wanted to focus on for our case studies, we struggled about the best way to get the real insider's story on what made these grants so special and then to find the best format for our readers. It would have been ideal to have everybody in the same room or even on the phone together for a free-flowing discussion, but given geography, different time zones, the fact that these are all very busy people, and the potential expense of such an endeavor, in the end we decided to interview each grantmaker and grantee separately by phone, but to ask them the same or very similar questions so that we could compare and contrast their responses. As you will see, the questions we asked quite closely align with the topics covered by the various chapters in this guide, and in much the same sequence. In each instance we recorded the conversation, transcribed the responses, and ran the final case study write-up by the interviewee for approval.

It might have made for a better story if the two individuals most involved with each grant disagreed on some important aspect of what actually occurred, but that was not what happened. As already indicated, despite not conferring with one another in advance, what we heard with the thee pairs and in all six interviews had marked similarity (in more than one instance the program officer and nonprofit staffer used almost exactly the same terminology and expressed identical opinions about the same issue), making us think that we may really have hit on some of the key components that lead to success in stewardship of foundation funds. Those have been outlined above.

At the conclusion of each case study interview we asked the individual for advice for the novice grantee. Some of what they said has been touched on already. The key words of advice can be summarized as follows:

- Stay in touch with your funder, but do so with a frequency and in a format that the funder prefers.

- Share both good and bad news. Don't be afraid to call on your foundation program officer for input when unexpected things happen. Each funder expressed the view that that's what they're there for.

- Find ways to be of service to your funder beyond simply carrying out the grant project (although that's important too). Don't contact your program officer only when you need money.

- Appreciate your funder; give credit where credit is due; invite your program officer to events.

- Complete the project as you said you would, according to the time frame you had originally agreed upon.

The case studies

In the case studies that follow you will learn more about each individual grant in the words of the experts—the foundation program officers and nonprofit grantees who were most involved in bringing them to fruition.

CASE STUDY 1

The Community Foundation for Greater Atlanta's Grant of $25,000 to Georgia Appleseed
March 2006–March 2007

The Community Foundation for Greater Atlanta, Atlanta, GA
Contact: Kathy Palumbo, MSW, PhD, Director of Community Partnerships
With over $770 million in assets, the foundation is one of the largest community foundations in the nation. Founded in 1951, the foundation assists donors and their families and works with nonprofit partners in 23 counties in the greater Atlanta area. The foundation helps people create donor-advised funds ranging from $50,000 to $18 million and currently serves as the charitable giving partner for 650 donors and their families.

Georgia Appleseed, Atlanta, GA
Contact: Theresa Brower, MSW, Deputy Director
Georgia Appleseed's mission: To listen to the unheard voices of the poor, the children, the marginalized; to uncover and end the injustices that we would not endure ourselves; to win the battles for our constituency in the courts of public opinion or in the halls of justice that no one else is willing or able to fight.

THE GRANT PROJECT: The Community Foundation for Greater Atlanta awarded $25,000 to Georgia Appleseed toward salaries of a Project Manager and the Executive Director for a project aimed at securing passage of a comprehensive revision of Georgia's juvenile justice code.

Could you say very briefly what this grant is really about?

Brower: The project is a revision of Georgia's twenty-five-year-old juvenile justice code in a way that will lead to better outcomes for children. It's very difficult for those in the field to use it in its current form, and as a result children are unnecessarily realizing poor outcomes. Nor does the current code reflect relevant scientific findings and best practices in the child development field. Legislation was introduced this past session in the Georgia legislature with strong support, and we hope that it will be passed next session.

Our part in the project was to determine what the status of juvenile justice is in Georgia. We recruited more than 260 attorneys to collect information around the state through interviews with a wide variety of stakeholders including judges, police officers, educators, and parents to gain their perspective on what was working, what wasn't working, and what needed to be changed about the state code. After conducting those interviews, we gathered the information and produced ten reports, one for each judicial district, as well as a statewide summary report. Then those reports were mailed to state legislators, judges, and other stakeholders.

GRANT AWARD NOTIFICATION

How was the grantee first alerted that the grant had been awarded?

Palumbo: We do a grant award letter in which we spell out what the award is for. We also include the amount of the grant and the grant's objectives. We attached a grant agreement that Georgia Appleseed's executive director and the board chair signed and then sent back to us.

Brower: We received a letter in the mail.

Were there any surprises in the actual grant award letter?

Palumbo: No, since we take the objectives verbatim from the proposal. If there were negotiations that we would have liked to have made, we would have done that during the site visit prior to giving the award.

Brower: Well, we were very pleased, in part because $25,000 is the maximum amount that the Community Foundation gives. And frequently they do not give out the maximum amount. [Editor's note: At the time $25,000 was the maximum; it has changed since then.] To us it was as much a vote of confidence in our work, as was receiving the grant money. Everything was as we expected.

MANAGING THE GRANT PROJECT

As the grant project unfolded, how close would you say the actual implementation was to what was described in the proposal?

Palumbo: I would say that it exceeded what was originally described in the proposal. Georgia Appleseed found good volunteers and educated those volunteers about the issue. Then they had those volunteers go out in the community and educate lay people about the issue. In doing so, they made the issue of the need to reform the juvenile code in the state one of public conversation.

Brower: I would say it was very close. This was really a well-thought well educated out project from the get-go with people who had experience doing this type of work. We laid the groundwork ahead of time. We put a lot of effort into planning at the very beginning, and it was a collaborative effort among the organizations. There weren't any surprises.

What systems did the grantee have in place that enabled it to effectively manage the grant funds?

Palumbo: I think Georgia Appleseed's staff is superb. They're well educated about the issues. They're well connected with the networks necessary to get this work done. They have a board that has the same sort of skill set in terms of social and professional networks, and legal expertise. They discovered a way to get this issue across to their target population, which was the legal community, because of who they were and how they did their work. The board that put this group together did that very well.

Brower: It took a lot of effort. Our executive director is a former juvenile court judge with connections in law firms and the juvenile court system, so she was key to making this happen. We could not have done this with a different executive director. We also have a very high-powered board with vast expertise in the field of law. In addition, some of those board members have been involved in the juvenile justice issues for quite some time.

COMMUNICATION

During the year of the grant project, how frequent would you say your communication was?

Palumbo: I think relatively frequent, both formally and informally. We would run into each other. And they're really good about electronic communication. They have an excellent web site and an excellent newsletter. We would check the web site periodically. It's part of our responsibility to stay on top of how organizations are doing, and if we can do that in a way that's not intrusive and doesn't take up their staff time, then we believe we should do that. In addition, Sharon Hill, the executive director, and Theresa came in several times during the year just to talk.

Brower: Since this project involves a collaboration among three groups, one of our partners is responsible for the public awareness aspect of the project, which helped to keep the community foundation informed. Our partners maintain a web site, JUSTGeorgia, as a way to keep the public informed. We also update our own web site with information about this project and others with which we are involved.

That said, we did communicate with the community foundation directly to keep them up to speed on our work related to this project. Additionally, we let them know about any of our events that are taking place. In addition to our normal fundraising events, which funders can come to free of charge, we have "friendraisers," in which we update our supporters on our current activities. We communicated by e-mail and requested a meeting with them to update them on the outcomes of the project, to let them know how we wanted to proceed with an additional part of the project, and to get their thoughts on it. Finally, we submitted an end-of-year grant report.

MEETINGS

How many site visits did you conduct for this particular grant and who attended?

Palumbo: We do one site visit related to each application we review. Georgia Appleseed doesn't provide direct services, so there was no program to view in action. We met in one of the big law firms here in town, which is a strong supporter. It was a little different than going to the "Boys & Girls Club"; yet it was a nice site visit. The chair of Georgia Appleseed's board came, and they conducted the meeting very well.

Brower: They made one site visit, which was extensive. We're housed in a law firm, so there's really nothing to see. They are very thorough in their interviews. The community foundation required that our board chair be there. They also wanted the executive director there, and, of course, myself.

LESSONS LEARNED

Was there a formal or informal evaluation of this particular grant project?

Palumbo: There was no formal evaluation. We mostly wanted to know about the outcomes Georgia Appleseed said it would achieve. When you look at the amount of this grant award, to ask an organization to do – or for us to invest additional time in doing – an intensive evaluation would be half the cost of the grant. We trust them enough to give them money; I think we trust them enough to report faithfully to us.

Brower: Not for this specific grant. It's really hard to evaluate policy work. It's a difficult thing to do. We do have our benchmarks. We said we'd interview these people, we'd produce these reports, we'd disseminate these reports to a certain number of people, and that's how we benchmark ourselves. Eventually, the test will be to see if the legislation is passed. The reality is that there will probably be compromises, so we'll also be looking at how much of it gets passed. Hopefully, we will know that in March 2010.

GRANT REPORT(S)

Were there interim and final reports with specific reporting requirements or formats?

Palumbo: We ask all our organizations to complete an end-of-grant report. Then I review them, and if there are questions that emerge from those reports, we ask for more information. It's also one of the pieces that we use if we get a consecutive application from the organization. It tells us: 1) Did they report? 2) Did they report on the outcomes that we supported? 3) Are they timely with the report? 4) Is the text describing the project informative?

Brower: We did a final report for them according to their guidelines, which are very specific. I would prefer more of a free-flowing format myself. It can be a little challenging to fill in the boxes with the word limit requirements. I don't know that you can always explain to the extent that you want to on one of these forms. However, it wasn't problematic, and I understand why they do that.

THE NEXT GRANT

Has the foundation awarded renewal funding for this project or funded other programs?

Palumbo: Yes, we gave a grant for a project manager for the collaboration as well as for some advocacy training. In addition, we are considering funding Georgia Appleseed for general operating support.

Brower: We actually have a general operating grant request under consideration with the community foundation right now. They just switched to awarding only general operating support this spring.

THE SUCCESSFUL GRANT PROJECT

What do you think it is about this particular grant project that makes it a good model for others to know about and emulate?

Palumbo: Well, number one, there's the end product. This will have an impact on every single family in the state of Georgia. To be a part of it with the limited size grants that we made at that time is pretty big leverage for us. So that's a good sell. And the methodical plan that they had for how to pursue this goal was key. It wasn't, "we're going to change the law, we're going to write a new bill." They were very systematic about what was going to be necessary to do this work. It doesn't mean that everything that they intended worked out, or that they haven't hit some roadblocks. But they knew what their goal was; they knew it was going to take a long time; they knew what the process was likely to be; and they were willing to do the work incrementally.

Brower: The funder was savvy, knowledgeable, and aware enough to understand the need to do policy work, because that's a hard sell for a lot of foundations. There aren't a lot of foundations out there funding policy work. In addition, we were able to put in action and leverage the legal services community. Not every organization can go out and do that. That's what we were able to bring to the table: we brought our core competencies into play with very little funding.

ADVICE TO A GRANTEE

If you were to give one piece of advice to a first-time grantee, what would be the best thing that she or he could do to ensure a productive relationship with a funder moving forward?

Palumbo: Be candid. If something changes, let us know. If something doesn't work, let us know. If something is wonderful, let us know. But always, always be candid. The times when we are disappointed are when someone told us X, and we found out that it was really Y. Then it's really hard then to look at the next application from that organization. For us, that's all about stewardship: to be accountable and to be candid.

Brower: You have to always be a good steward of that money. People are putting their trust in you to use their grant funds wisely. Don't ever lose sight of the fact that you have to be accountable for how you spend their money and the trust they put in you to use it as you said you would.

CASE STUDY 2

The S. H. Cowell Foundation's Grant of $23,000 to On the Move
March 2006–March 2007

The S. H. Cowell Foundation, San Francisco, CA
Contact: Jamie Allison, Program Officer, Youth Development
The goal of the S. H. Cowell Foundation is to improve the quality of life of children and families living in Northern and Central California by making grants that directly support and strengthen children, families, and the neighborhoods where they live. Priority is given to communities where Cowell has made, or could make, place-based complementary grants in Northern and Central California towns and neighborhoods where there is widespread and acute poverty and there are strong working relationships among residents and institutional leaders. The foundation funds efforts to increase a town's or neighborhood's capacity to engage and serve its low-income families.

On the Move, Napa, CA
Contact: Leslie Medine, Executive Director
On the Move is a nonprofit organization that promotes vibrant communities by building and sustaining effective leaders and highly functional organizations within the public sector. V.O.I.C.E.S. unites transitioning foster youth, social service agencies, educational institutions, and committed community members to help young people become independent adults and engaged citizens.

THE GRANT PROJECT: In 2006, the S. H. Cowell Foundation awarded $23,000 to On the Move for its V.O.I.C.E.S. program.

Could you say very briefly what this grant is really about?

Allison: I would say there are three things. One is that the grant, or the proposal, was about doing something new and innovative. It was about serving foster youth in a different way than is typical in the child welfare system.

The second piece was that it was an interesting program that helped young people gain leadership skills and helped them take responsibility for their well-being and for their futures and partnering with adults, which is a tool or method in youth development that we value here at the foundation.

And the third is that Leslie Medine, who is the founder and director of On the Move, was also proposing that she would be coordinating her work in a place-based strategy, which closely aligns with how the foundation carries out its work. We look to make clusters of grants across all our program areas in a single community. On the Move, in addition to having this innovative way of providing services to foster youth who were about to emancipate or emancipated already and helping young people gain leadership skills and take responsibility for their future, also proposed that part of this work would help ground them in a specific community where they hoped to develop other programs and initiatives that would support the community where V.O.I.C.E.S. would be located.

Medine: Number one, it was place-based, which is the direction Cowell was going, meaning that we were going to be focused on one area in Napa. Number two, this was sort of a hybrid grant, because on the one hand it was place-based, but on the other hand it was for youth development, which of course they're also interested in. And thirdly, they also have an interest in leadership development, generally speaking. This grant really combines all three things. Specifically in youth development, Cowell was really interested in the fact that the center we were proposing to open was going to be youth-led.

GRANT AWARD NOTIFICATION

How was the grantee first alerted that the grant had been awarded?

Allison: I can't remember if Leslie picked up the phone that day I called her. But if I call someone and they don't answer the phone, then I put everything in an e-mail. I say, "Hey, congratulations, I'm really excited. You've been awarded this grant, here's why. You're going to get these documents in the mail; please sign them. Call me at your earliest convenience so that we can talk it through, in case you have any questions." I would have told her that she would get the check in the mail along with the grant agreement that we ask that she sign and return a copy to us.

Medine: Cowell would have called. That's how they normally do things, and then they send a letter later.

Had there been a lot of back and forth by phone, by e-mail, or in person leading up to the actual grant award?

Allison: The proposal that On the Move submitted was the second draft, if not the third. The first conversation would have taken place before there was a written proposal. We would have been talking about the ideas. Then there would have been a draft where I gave feedback, and we had another conversation. We talked about the proposal and refined it based on what I felt like I was hearing On the Move say they wanted the Cowell Foundation to fund.

Once we had a proposal that we felt clearly and accurately described the project and the request to Cowell, I wrote a cover memo that explained my recommendation and why I thought the foundation should fund it. Because my recommendation doesn't necessarily repeat what's in the proposal, sometimes I go back to the grantee for accuracy. I say: "I'm going to say this thing about you and what you're doing. Is this true?" So there would have been some conversations about my write-up as well before submitting it.

Medine: Let me say, I have probably 37 different funders, currently, and over the years I've had many other funders. S. H. Cowell is very specific, and Lise in particular, is very particular about exactly what she wants and exactly how she wants the grant to look. There's never anything gray, or fuzzy, or "Oh, I thought you meant…" It just doesn't happen with Cowell.

Were there any surprises in the actual grant award letter?

Allison: I don't think so, because I would have called Leslie to let her know that the grant award had been approved.

Medine: No, it was very similar to what was in the actual proposal.

MANAGING THE GRANT PROJECT

As the grant project unfolded, how close would you say the actual implementation was to what was described in the proposal?

Allison: It was almost exactly if not exactly what was described. I would say the only difference is that On the Move exceeded the objectives they had laid out. They did more than they said they would do.

Medine: It was exactly the same, except that we did more than we were supposed to. We exceeded our objectives.

What systems did the grantee have in place that enabled it to effectively manage the grant funds?

Allison: I can't answer that precisely, but what I can say is that On the Move has a director of operations and finance. She is responsible for helping to make sure that I get whatever financial reports I need. I think having a person on staff whose sole responsibility is some of the back office administration activities as opposed to having someone who is responsible for programs also be responsible for administrative tasks is really helpful.

Medine: I have a grants manager who helps move the pieces around, making sure the funder is getting everything they need, and keeping track of when everything is due, and all that stuff. So I have a part-time grants manager for that. That's one. Number two, 50 percent of my time is spent on fund development. That's my job. And thirdly, I have an excellent CFO who makes sure all the financials, the use of the funds, the reporting of the funds, all of that is in place.

COMMUNICATION

During the year of the grant project, how frequent would you say your communication was?

Allison: It was not excessive. This particular project was only one year long. After the grant had been approved, we had some communications about the ongoing process. Since things were going so well when the progress report was submitted, there wasn't necessarily any reason to have more frequent contact. I will say, though, that the project did get quite a bit of media attention. Leslie or someone on her staff was always very good about sending those media pieces to me so that I would know what was happening out in the community.

Medine: I'm sure at the mid-year point we had a conversation about the report and how everything was going. We had a huge amount of media coverage for this project. Any time we got media coverage, we sent them copies.

What form did the communication usually take?

Allison: The media pieces usually came via e-mail. If there were ever any special events going on, I would get e-mails about them. Then someone from On the Move's staff would also call and let me know that the event was going to take place. For example, there was a grand opening. I would have gotten an invitation via e-mail, and then someone would call and say, "Jamie, we're having this event on this day. Can you make it?"

Medine: Because I have a relationship with Cowell, when good stuff happened, which was a lot of the time on this project, I would call and have a conversation with them about how it was going. There was a lot of good news to report.

MEETINGS

How many site visits did you conduct for this particular grant?

Allison: There was a face-to-face meeting with Leslie and me here in the Cowell office, which I would count as a site visit. And then I also met with her at another foundation's office where she was, not exactly pitching, but at least describing the V.O.I.C.E.S. work and their leadership development model where there were lots of other funders that were invited. And then I also visited the young people who were the co-founders of V.O.I.C.E.S. with Leslie.

Medine: That is a great question. I believe that because it was so new, there wasn't anything there yet. We didn't do a site visit beforehand, but I know they did several site visits over the years. During that first year, one of them must have come to the grand opening, which was right around November. And over the years, every time they're up here for something else, they come and visit.

LESSONS LEARNED

Was there a formal or informal evaluation of this particular grant project?

Allison: I would say no, other than the regular reporting that was required. I did read the reports and assess them against the original intent of the project. In addition, once the grant file was closed, I was responsible for doing a grant assessment to determine if the grant project fulfilled the deliverables.

Medine: Not on this grant. This grant was so small and straightforward that you could see the objectives written on the proposal, and we just reported on them.

GRANT REPORT(S)

Were there interim and final reports with specific reporting requirements or formats?

Allison: Yes, for this grant there were interim and final reports. There's no specific format. However, included in the award documents and contract, there is a section that describes the information that we expect the grantee to report on. Those deliverables are usually determined between Cowell and the grantee before the proposal is submitted. Their report contained a good balance of describing the activities that went on as well as taking the extra step to conduct a higher-level analysis and ask, "What does all this mean?"

Medine: Yes, there were interim and final reports. The format was very informal. Cowell wanted to know, "Did you meet the objectives? How was it? What challenges did you face? What did you learn?" The challenges and lessons learned are very important to them.

THE NEXT GRANT

Has the foundation awarded renewal funding for this project or funded other programs?

Allison: We are funding other elements of On the Move's programming. Another program that On the Move runs is called the Leadership Academy. It's a leadership development program primarily for high school students, but middle school and elementary students take part as well. Now the Cowell Foundation supports the Leadership Academy work.

Medine: Not on this particular grant. When we did this grant, Cowell specifically said, "This is a one-year grant. It's sort of unusual, and we really just want to support this effort." I never did reapply there. But currently they support a lot of our other work in Napa.

THE SUCCESSFUL GRANT PROJECT

What do you think it is about this particular grant project that makes it a good model for others to know about and emulate?

Allison: Some of the things I think we've covered already: There was a lot of contact between the grantee and Cowell prior to the submission of the proposal. During the development of the proposal there were opportunities for me to give feedback before the final proposal was submitted to the foundation. I think that early and frequent contact helped us to be clear with each other about our expectations. I think that the regular and informal updates helped keep the project in the front of my mind, and to be aware of the progress the grantee was making, even when it wasn't necessarily time for a report. Getting the e-mails of the media coverage or finding out that there was a particular event going on helped me see that there was activity, momentum, and support in the community for what they were doing. And those things weren't necessarily part of the grant deliverables.

I should say that part of the success, at least in terms of the relationship that Cowell developed with On the Move, is that the grant to V.O.I.C.E.S. laid the groundwork or the platform to think about other ways to support On the Move's work in this specific community. In addition to visiting V.O.I.C.E.S. specifically for site visits relating to the Cowell Foundation grant, the foundation was also invited by On the Move to view the broader community place-based work that it was going to engage in.

Medine: Number one, because Lise and I had worked together for a number of years, I knew that she had appreciated and funded youth-led work. Part of the relationship with her was that I knew I was asking her for something that she really believed in. And number two, she was really familiar with us because we had done many other youth-led initiatives before this one. I try to spend a lot of time up front with the funder trying to figure out whether or not this is a good fit instead of trying to push it. If it's a good fit, we'll move forward. If it doesn't make sense, for whatever reason, then there's no point trying to push through something. I knew when I approached Cowell that they had a deep understanding of what we were trying to do.

Also, both of us knew that the chance of this project having great widespread media coverage—locally, regionally, and nationally—was going to be really good. It's always important to a funder—and a foundation board in particular—that they get to say, "Hey, we were there in the beginning."

And I think the third thing is that Lise and I had done start-ups before. Not every funder wants to be involved in the beginning when it's never been there before.

Because Cowell had been there with me in other start-ups, she had a sense that her board would go along with something that was a start-up, something innovative and new. And the other thing was, for Cowell, $25,000 is a very small amount. It wasn't a high-risk, high-stakes grant.

ADVICE TO THE GRANTEE

If you were to give one piece of advice to a first-time grantee, what would be the best thing that she or he could do to ensure a productive relationship with a funder moving forward?

Allison: I would say if there is any problem or hint of a problem to let your program officer know immediately. Don't be shy. I think sometimes grantees think that the foundation wants them to be perfect all the time, and if we hear that there's a problem, we'll get upset and rescind the grant. That's absolutely not the case. We know that sometimes things don't go according to plan, and we'd like to know about that sooner rather than later. There's an opportunity for us to help, either with additional funding, or connecting the person to some kind of technical assistance provider, or just thinking through the problem over the phone. That's what program officers do. That's our job, and we're happy to do it. That kind of honesty helps to build trust in the relationship, so that when the grantee applies to the foundation again, we know, hey, this person came to us when there was a situation that was embarrassing to him or her. We can trust this person. As a grantee, you have to be very brave.

Medine: A few things: One would be to stay in regular contact about the good news. Keep the funder posted. Don't send them an e-mail every five minutes, but keep them apprised as to the good stuff going on. Number two, whenever possible try to get the name of the funder out there and try to get your funders connected to each other. And I think the third thing is to utilize your funders in terms of content expertise. When I'm having trouble or worried about something, or something feels like it's falling apart, then I call up and ask for their advice.

Also, if something is not going right, or even if I'm just worried, I'm very transparent and upfront and direct about telling them. I might say: these six things were incredible, and these two things were just absolutely off the wall. This is what we thought was going to happen, but this is in fact what happened. My experience with funders is that they are much more interested in what isn't working. Because when we're learning something about what we thought was going to work and it didn't, they can use that to inform the field or other grantees. It's not interesting for me to tell them that all 28 things went right. Fine, those things happened. But more importantly, what didn't go right, what did you learn, and what would you do differently next time? That's the really interesting conversation. And I think that lots of grantees, and I would assume especially new ones, would be really worried about telling a funder the truth about either how hard it is or how challenging or about something that didn't work.

CASE STUDY 3

Charles Stewart Mott Foundation's Grant of $300,000 to the Institute for Conservation Leadership
June 2007–June 2009

Charles Stewart Mott Foundation, Flint, MI
Contact: Sam Passmore, Program Director—Environment
The C.S. Mott Foundation supports efforts that promote a just, equitable, and sustainable society with the primary focus on civil society; the environment: the area of Flint, Michigan; and poverty. The foundation makes grants for a variety of purposes within these program areas including: philanthropy and voluntarism; assisting emerging civil societies in Central/Eastern Europe, Russia, and South Africa; conservation of freshwater ecosystems in North America; international finance for sustainability; reform of international finance and trade; improving the outcomes for children, youth, and families at risk of persistent poverty; education; and neighborhood and economic development. The foundation also makes grants to strengthen the capacity of local institutions in its home community of Flint, Michigan.

Institute for Conservation Leadership (ICL), Takoma Park, MD
Contact: Dianne Russell, Executive Director
The Institute for Conservation Leadership strengthens leaders, organizations, and coalitions or networks that protect and conserve the Earth. ICL uses the tools of consulting, training, coaching, meeting facilitation, and research to help groups more effectively accomplish their missions.

THE GRANT PROJECT: The C.S. Mott Foundation awarded $300,000 to the Institute for Conservation Leadership's Freshwater Leadership Initiative, which is an ongoing effort to provide organizational and leadership development support to groups in the Great Lakes region and in the southeast United States. The goal of the Freshwater Leadership Initiative is to strengthen organizations whose work has an impact on restoring and protecting freshwater ecosystems in these regions.

Could you say very briefly what this grant is really about?

Passmore: One of the objectives of the Mott Foundation's environmental program area is to build the organizational strength of the community of freshwater advocacy groups in our regions of interest. The Institute for Conservation Leadership provides capacity-building, technical assistance to this community of groups.

Russell: The banner for this project is the Freshwater Leadership Initiative. We provide capacity-building support to a wide variety of nonprofit leaders, organizations, and networks and coalitions involved in freshwater advocacy. The project is focused on leadership at all levels. We're very serious about building capacity that's going to last and have staying power.

The Institute engages with the organizations in four different ways. The first consists of limited engagements at workshops that we or a regional partner organization sponsors. The second way we engage with the organizations is through our Signature Intensive Programs. These are engagements with a group of leaders or a group of organizations that usually last from five to twelve months. The third category would be custom-designed coaching or consulting in support of that groups request. Then the fourth category would be one-on-one outreach meetings, which the Mott foundation encouraged us to do with their resources. That outreach has proven to be incredibly helpful for groups or leaders who are new to ICL and don't know the program options we provide.

GRANT AWARD NOTIFICATION

How was the grantee first alerted that the grant had been awarded?

Passmore: I almost always send an e-mail or call the grantee. When we learn internally that the grant award has been approved, we'll immediately let the grantee know—that's the best part of my job! About a week later the grantee will receive the grant commitment letter, which is essentially a contract that the grantee has to sign and return to us. We won't make the grant payment until we receive the signed commitment letter.

Russell: The Mott Foundation has always done a phone call followed by an official letter. I've always appreciated that.

Were there any surprises in the actual grant award letter?

Passmore: I doubt it, because we have a long relationship with the Institute for Conservation Leadership. Also, the Institute is pretty sophisticated about fundraising.

Russell: No, there weren't any surprises.

MANAGING THE GRANT PROJECT

As the grant project unfolded, how close would you say the actual implementation was to what was described in the proposal?

Passmore: I would say quite close. There's some flexibility built into the grant, so there was some shifting of priorities over the course of the grant period within the project's overall framework.

Russell: I would say the way we conducted it was probably about 85 percent of the way we had described it in the proposal. This is one of the rockiest climates we've ever seen. In addition, Mott shifted its funding priorities in the last six months of the grant. That has led to a number of conversations with Mott's grantees and other capacity builders serving those grantees about how we can best serve the groups who will no longer receive grants after 2010.

We've also noticed that it's harder for leaders to make time for workshops. As a result, we've been focusing on our distance learning offerings. We have moved to offering webinars and more distance learning. I think some of our numbers will be quite different from what we originally anticipated.

What systems did the grantee have in place that enabled it to effectively manage the grant funds?

Passmore: The Institute for Conservation Leadership has a very finely tuned expense tracking system. They track the dollars very closely and do very sophisticated budgeting. I think in part ICL is trying to "walk the talk," since they are out there telling other organizations how to manage themselves. At the same time, they have to track their gifts, since they have so little general support funding. Almost all their grant awards are for restricted project funding. In order to keep track of things, it really benefits them to have a good accounting system.

Russell: We have a very detailed fund-accounting program that allows us to track grant expenditures on a monthly basis. We focus specifically on expenditure of time. For our grants with Mott and a lot of other foundations, time is the biggest resource we have. One of the things I like about our careful accounting of funds and resources is that it allows us to match what we estimated with what we're delivering. Getting that kind of information allows us not only to report to Mott about our progress on the grant, but it also helps us do a better job budgeting for the next cycle. We've found that the fund accounting and the monthly time tracking systems allow us to anticipate when we need to modify activities. In addition, at a managerial level, our administrative director and I meet with the finance committee monthly to look at the financials for the whole organization. Our board is a model for governance, and the finance committee is just outstanding.

The second aspect of our systems is evaluation, and in particular getting direct feedback about the relevance of our programs. Some of our evaluation efforts are aimed at securing feedback directly from people who are using our services through our programs. We also ask our partners what they're hearing about our programs and what they're hearing about the programs' effectiveness.

COMMUNICATION

During the period of the grant project, how frequent would you say your communication was?

Passmore: The most formal way we communicated was through the interim grant report. Beyond that, we communicated by phone or e-mail. Sometimes I'll request a phone call if I hear something that either interests or concerns me. There were at least one or two occasions to connect by phone or in person through the course of the year. Since ICL is based in the Washington, D.C. area, it's not difficult for me to stop by their offices, if I'm in town for some other reason. The Institute will also get in touch with me. For instance, if they have any questions, they'll send an e-mail to me and say, "We're thinking of working with these ten groups. Any thoughts?"

Russell: We really tried to communicate as frequently as Mott would let us or told us that they wanted us to. We used a whole range of different communication formats, and we always received a prompt response. Most importantly, rather than just assuming that Sam shouldn't be bothered and should only get an e-mail, I never hesitated to pick up the phone if I thought that was a better way to communicate about what was going on. More often than not we try to send a quarterly update by e-mail rather than waiting until the report period was over. ICL would also check with Mott to make sure that the groups who signed up for our Signature Intensive Programs fit with Mott's idea of whom we should be serving. I just think that this kind of ongoing communication has really strengthened the relationship and made us more confident about decisions we're making.

MEETINGS

How many site visits did you conduct for this particular grant and who attended?

Passmore: We conduct at least one site visit during a grant period. Our most recent site visit took place earlier this year. I should note that the responsibility for the grant has shifted from me to a colleague. Part of the purpose of the site visit was to introduce my colleague to ICL's staff and to help with the transition. The Institute is an important grantee for us, so I wanted to make sure that the hand-off was handled well. We met with ICL's executive director, the project manager, and one other senior staff person who is involved in the project. We also had a specific question unrelated to the project that drew on their expertise, and another staff member called in for that part of the site visit.

Russell: Mott usually does a site visit once every two years, so once in a grant period. The site visits are usually three or four hours long. Mott comes in with a lot of questions, and they really push us to think. The in-depth conversation and the level of the questions they ask led to more productive work on our part moving forward.

We came out of the visit with a more nuanced understanding of what we should be doing with our programs as well as what we both were seeing with the groups and the leaders in the region.

LESSONS LEARNED

Was there a formal or informal evaluation of this particular grant project?

Passmore: This project has an evaluation component built into it, but the foundation doesn't require its grantees to retain an outside evaluator. Usually we ask the grantee how they plan to track progress and evaluate the impact of their work. In this case, ICL wanted to have a more rigorous evaluation component, and we were quite willing to support that. Over the years, the amount of resources devoted to evaluation has varied depending on the kind of questions ICL had about impact and whether or not they were on track. We really depend on the Institute to decide if they need to do a formal evaluation. But I think in every grant request, there's always been an item in the budget for them to hire an outside evaluator. In terms of evaluating the foundation's impact, we tend to focus more on clusters of grants that are part of a larger strategy, rather than individual projects such as ICL's Freshwater Leadership Initiative.

Russell: We had some limited external evaluation resources set aside for this project. We generally fluctuate in terms of how much external, formal evaluation we do. The Institute has very strong evaluation systems in place, and we use an external resource person for sampling and testing some of the more intensive work that we do. So for the most part we use our own evaluation data and run it against the objectives and outcomes stated in the grant proposal. On occasion we use external evaluators to look at our Signature Intensive Programs.

GRANT REPORT(S)

Were there interim and final reports with specific reporting requirements or formats?

Passmore: There was an interim report, which was due halfway through the grant, as well as a final report. When Mott receives the grant report, we review it, and then approve it. I always let the Institute know when the report has been approved, even if it's just a courtesy. If there are questions, I'll send ICL an e-mail, and they'll decide whether or not a phone call is needed. On a rare occasion there may be a question that needs to be answered before we approve the report. We don't release the next grant payment until the report is approved, so it's important to get questions answered as quickly as possible. If it's not a "showstopper" kind of question, I'll go ahead and approve the report and ask the question after the fact.

Russell: Yes, there were interim and final reports. The reports are really manageable, and I think Mott's requirements are very appropriate. Their requirements are very clear and very reasonable. I don't know how I would restructure it. I feel as if Mott asks all the right questions. In addition, reporting annually establishes a really good rhythm for us. It helps us pause and think about where we are and reframe what we're going to do for the next year.

THE NEXT GRANT

Has the foundation awarded renewal funding for this project or funded other programs?

Passmore: Yes, we've just awarded them another two-year grant.

Russell: Yes, we have an ongoing relationship with Mott, and we're starting a new grant cycle now.

THE SUCCESSFUL GRANT PROJECT

What do you think it is about this particular grant project that makes it a good model for others to know about and emulate?

Passmore: I think we at the Mott Foundation are pretty clear on what our grantmaking strategy is and why we think this project is consistent with our strategy. The Institute understands our grantmaking strategy and why we think what they're doing is in line with the kind of work we want to be supporting. I think that's one thing that helps.

The other thing is that ICL is a high performer. As a result, we've gotten to know the Institute well. It helps that there's been continuity in their leadership. One thing that characterizes this project as a success is that in the beginning the terms of the grant and the agreement were fairly well defined, and the deliverables were quite specific. But as Mott has gotten to know ICL, and they've gotten to know us, both parties' understanding of what Mott is trying to accomplish via its grantmaking has improved. And more flexibility has been introduced into the scope of the grant. The Institute has a lot more latitude now than they did on day one.

Russell: One of the richest aspects of working with Mott is that the concept and the work match our sense of what is needed by the groups and the leaders we're seeking to serve. The Mott Foundation's knowledge of working with those grantees and what their needs are is folded into what we've learned from working with those groups on the ground. We feel as if we're really in partnership with Mott. We're both highly committed to building the capacity of the groups, so that Freshwater work will continue for a very long time.

In addition, Mott has given us the freedom and confidence to do our work in the best way we can. We, in turn, have tried hard to respect the foundation's culture, its ways, its needs, and its network. One of my colleagues is fond of saying, "If you've met one foundation, you've met one foundation." I think that's absolutely true. Mott has done us a favor by saying, "If you've met one provider of capacity-building services, you've met one provider of capacity-building services." They've really enabled us to shine. I think a lot of foundations get boxed in by their own trustees, or by their singular requirements, or by their geographic restrictions or by the kinds of groups they're willing to help. Mott, in contrast, has allowed us to serve a broad range of groups working on Freshwater with a whole variety of tools that we have in our toolbox.

ADVICE TO A GRANTEE

If you were to give one piece of advice to a first-time grantee, what would be the best thing that she or he could do to ensure a productive relationship with a funder moving forward?

Passmore: Ask the program officer what he or she wants in terms of reporting on the grant: What level of detail? Would he or she prefer it in writing or by phone? Or would he or she like you to come by some time? Each program officer is different and will have different appetites for different levels of information conveyed in different ways. A foundation of Mott's size has certain reporting procedures and so on, but there's still a lot of latitude and flexibility that is left to the program officer. And somebody in this kind of position has a lot of stuff coming at them all the time, so it's really in the grantee's best interest to make it as easy as possible. Also, once you ask one of these questions, listen carefully to the response, and then do exactly what the person says. I've had situations where the question has been asked, and I've been very, very clear, and then I'll get back something completely different than what I asked for.

Russell: The number one thing to do is to appreciate your funder for who they are and what their mission is in the world. Say thank you when they call, and when they help, especially in non-monetary ways. There's a lot of things that funders can do for grantees that don't involve writing a check or asking about progress on a project. Saying thank you whenever help is provided is at the top of my list.

The second thing to do is to communicate as often as the foundation permits. Be honest about what's going on at your organization. Don't try to hide information that you ascertain from your evaluation because you're trying to look good. But also don't be afraid of looking good if the evaluation data that you're getting indicates that. If there is a problem, you don't want your program officer to find out about it for the first time when he or she reads the grant report. When you're completely honest with your funder, it helps them trust you even more.

The final thing I would say is to look for ways to be of service to the foundation, not just in delivering the project or the work under the grant, but in ways that will show that you are a resource to the broader community or on the issue that you're addressing. You come to the relationship as an expert, and the foundation brings its own expertise. The trick is to match expertise, opinions, and experience in such a way that you create something that really serves both the grantee's and the funder's interests.

Appendix A—Troubleshooting Guide

Marilyn Hoyt

Your proposal was built around a particular need and your organization's response to it. It included a budget indicating quite specifically how funds will be allocated to meet that need. And it talked about key people who will lead and carry out the work it describes in some detail. All of these components were reviewed by the foundation decision maker prior to the grant award, and all of them are important aspects of your relationship with your funder going forward. And behind this effort stand your CEO and board of trustees.

After the grant award, during the course of the year, things change. Sometimes these changes are positive, and you have the pleasure of communicating good news to your funder. (And do be sure to do that! It is their success too and is the most powerful way to strengthen your relationship.)

With this troubleshooting guide, however, we address changes after the grant award that may not be particularly good news for you or for the funder. When these things happen, as other authors have emphasized in various ways throughout this guide, it is especially critical to keep your foundation funder "in the loop." Doing so effectively prevents minor problems in your relationship with your funder from turning into major difficulties and can actually strengthen your partnership for the future.

Below you will find some of the more common unanticipated changes and sensitive issues that may arise over the course of the grant period and some solid advice on how to respond. To further elaborate on the advice we provide here, we have polled colleagues on both sides of the grantmaker/grantee equation. Select quotes from these conversations are provided to underscore the points being made.

Changes at your organization

Q. What if the project leader leaves your organization mid-grant?

A. If your project leader had a relationship with the foundation program officer or was uniquely qualified and well known in the field, you need to call the program officer, tell him or her about the departure, and introduce the individual who will be taking up the reins, or explain how and when the project leader will be replaced. In other instances, however, a change in staffing (not the project leadership) is part of the normal ongoing work of your organization and no special calls need to be made. Noting the change in your interim or final report on the grant may be all that is required.

Effective grantmaking is fundamentally about authenticity. So when people change, and the people who knew this was coming don't communicate, the authenticity of the whole relationship can be called into question.

> —Leonard Aube, Managing Director, Annenberg Foundation, Los Angeles

Q. What if your CEO changes during the grant period?

A. This is the change foundations tend to care about most. As soon as you know this change is going to take place (ideally you should have some lead time), make separate lists of those funders that need a phone call from the person who manages the relationship and those that should receive a letter signed by your board chair.

Both forms of communication will state that the current CEO is leaving (without providing a great deal of detail on the reasons for this departure) and lay out the plan for interim leadership, if necessary, as well as the search process and timeline for the CEO's replacement. If appropriate, you should ask for your funder's feedback and advice. Most foundation staff members have witnessed a lot of transitions and may have tips on handling them well. They may even know of appropriate candidates for the position. Let them know that you'll be back in touch when the new CEO is identified.

Communication between funder and grantees doesn't only revolve around a specific grant request. If it is an important and longstanding relationship, communicating with your funder about important organizational changes—such as leadership changes—is very much appreciated by funders. That kind of communication goes a long way toward solidifying relationships and helping funders feel that they are important stakeholders in the organization.

> —Janet Sarbaugh, Senior Director, Heinz Endowments, Pittsburgh

Q. What if your board chair changes during the grant period?

A. In the first place, this may not necessarily be bad news. In fact, it may present an excuse to contact your foundation program officer with some positive communication. However, if your board chair has a close relationship with a foundation or is well known or highly identified with your organization (or if that individual played a prominent role in a site visit with the funding representative), then you should communicate this change in the same manner you use when the CEO changes, as noted above.

The key is an active and engaged board. The board needs to show leadership by managing staff, monitoring resources, and planning for succession. If the board is strong, the organization can better prepare to face challenging times.
—Michelle Boone, Program Officer, The Joyce Foundation, Chicago

Changes in timing and reallocation of budgeted grant funds

Q. What if your fiscal year does not correspond with the grant award year?

A. Sometimes timing issues come up because your fiscal year and the grant award year do not match. And when your new fiscal year starts, the budget for the project or even the budget for the entire organization may be somewhat different. If the intent and execution of the funded activity are basically the same, you can report minor budget reallocations in the next report you submit to the funder. But if the scope of the funded project changes significantly, see troubleshooting advice provided below. Ideally, when you first received the grant award letter you would have taken note of a potential conflict between the foundation's expectations as to timing and your organization's ability to deliver and report back in light of your fiscal year, and you would have already addressed this issue with your funder before proceeding with the grant-funded project.

Q. What if the grant year is over, but the full grant amount has not yet been spent?

A. In these circumstances, you have two choices:

Option 1: Confer with your financial staff or whoever handles your books, and ask that individual to document which funds have been used to offset program expenses in this fiscal year. If income from an unrestricted grant or one that concludes later in the year was used to offset program expenses applicable to your current grant, your finance staff, with the approval of the administrator responsible for signing off on program expenses, can transfer income from one category to another, thus releasing the unrestricted or other grant income to be utilized against some other expenses of your organization's programs at a later date.

There is a preventative for this problem: monthly monitoring. The grantee's program and finance staff should collaborate in this process. All expenditures should be reviewed, in detail, against the approved grant budget. The grantee's accounting software should accommodate detailed line, project, and donor account classification. Program staff who authorize expenditures should be thoroughly familiar with the approved grant budget. If a smaller grantee cannot manage tracking income and expense for specific grants, it may make sense to get a conduit organization or fiscal agent involved to receive, track, and report on the grant.

—Jane Dunne, Not-for-Profit Consultant, New York

Option 2: Contact your foundation program officer. Let him or her know that your grant is not yet fully expended and explain the reason why. Keep in mind that it is required by audit standards for restricted fund accounting and, of course, in the funders' interest to see that the grant they awarded is applied to the services they intended to support. It's the nonprofit organization's job to make sure grant funds are spent appropriately. Failure to properly supervise allocation of funds is not a viable reason to request an extension. Assuming you have a valid excuse (and there can be many that are legitimate), ask for a reasonable, additional period of time in which to complete the work funded by the grant and an extension on the due date for the final report. Offer to submit an interim report or informal update. Most funders will agree to this request.

A good program officer should know what the grantee is doing and doesn't want any surprises. If there have been changes in the circumstances, opportunities, or other factors that would influence the conduct of a grant, it is important for the grantee to be very straightforward and honest about them. If the grantee needs or wants to extend the grant period due to minor issues that do not substantially change the nature or duration of grant-funded activities, a simple extension might be possible. However, if the changes require a significant extension or restructuring of the grant, then we would ask for a written plan and discuss this with the grantee.

—Suzanne Siskel, Director, Social Justice Philanthropy, Ford Foundation, New York

The funder does not want the money back. Funding organizations want the projects to procceed as planned. Depending on the guidelines, a timeline extension may be granted, but the applicant should call and/or submit a letter requesting such to the funder. A written request provides transparency to both parties and provides evidence from which a grantor can then follow up as needed.

—Mark Fraire, Grant Programs Specialist, Wisconsin Arts Board, Madison

Q. What if the grant money was spent on items not specifically covered by the funded project?

A. This is a definite "no-no" when building a relationship with a foundation. It may be one of the worst things you can do, and clearly indicates to the funder that your organization is not fiscally responsible and may even be poorly run. In other words, it represents the essence of poor stewardship of a foundation's grant funds. Since your reputation is paramount when it comes to partnering with foundations, you want to avoid this mistake at all costs. Accounting standards for nonprofit organizations simply do not allow you to spend restricted money under a grant as though it were unrestricted income.

If the cash from the grant is spent, but the funded activity has not been performed and no expenditures have been incurred on the grant, the financial statements will reflect the grant in the temporarily restricted net assets category. In addition, additional disclosures in the financial statements may be necessary if the organization does not have sufficient resources to comply with the grant agreement. The foundation should be informed of the situation as soon as possible to avoid potential relationship problems and noncompliance with the terms of the agreement.
   —Kim Johnson, Partner and Group Leader of KPMG's New York Nonprofit Practice

Q. What if you receive a grant for general operating support; can you spend it on anything you want?

A. From the standpoint of accepted financial practices and your auditors, yes, you can spend these funds on anything you want, as long as they relate to the operation of your nonprofit. However, from the standpoint of your relationship with the foundation, you may want to refer back to your original proposal as you move forward expending the grant funds, and certainly before you issue your final report. Your general operating support proposal may have talked about your organization in terms of a set of programs meeting specific needs. It probably described the work of your organization as a whole and may have identified particular constituencies that would benefit from the grant. If there have been significant changes in your mission, your constituency, or the scope of your activities, be sure that your report makes very clear the connections between what you originally proposed (and what the foundation thought it was supporting) and what has transpired since then.

Q. What if a funder gives you less than you asked for, and consequently you do not have enough money to accomplish what you described in the grant proposal?

A. It is in fact unusual for a single funder to provide all of the monies needed for a grantee's program. Ideally you would have already asked a number of funders to support the program or various components of it, or will have a list of potential funders waiting in the wings. When you receive far less than you need, check first to see if you can approach other funders on your prospect list to make up for the partial funding needed.

If it appears that additional funding cannot be raised for the program in a timely manner, call the funder that gave your organization less than requested. Let the program officer know how much you appreciate the funding they provided, but be frank about your ability to accomplish only part of what was set out in the original proposal. Then discuss a plan to move at least some aspects of the program forward with the funding at hand. Since most likely the funder will not want their money back, this discussion should be all that is required. The program officer may, however, request that you submit a revised budget and program narrative. Or if you're lucky, he or she may even recommend or offer to introduce you to other funders to help support the program.

Grantmaker relationships and communication

Q. What if your program officer changes in the middle of your grant period?

A. In today's philanthropic world, such changes happen frequently. Some of the larger foundations even have policies in place about how long a particular staff member can work in a given program area. If possible, assuming you hear about this change in advance, you should be in touch with your original program officer before he or she leaves the post. Thank this individual for the work you have accomplished together and wish the person well. If it is known, determine the name of the program officer you will be working with in the future, and ask for an introduction to that individual. A joint meeting between you and the two of them to "pass the baton" would be ideal, but is not always possible. Since it is common for program officers to move from foundation to foundation, you may well benefit from having your "old" program officer became a "new" program officer at another foundation with priorities that match your mission, thus opening up the potential for a brand-new funding source for your organization.

I call as soon as I hear that my program officer is leaving. I want to thank them, find out where they are moving to, just in case there's a good fit for us at this new foundation, and determine whether they know who is handling our account at the old foundation. Over the years I've seen a lot of program officers move from one foundation to another. Sometimes this has opened the door for a first grant.
—Terry Billie, Assistant VP Institutional Advancement, New York Hall of Science

Q. How do you introduce yourself to a new program officer taking over your funding area at a foundation?

A. Once you know the name of the individual you'll be building a new relationship with, send him or her a note of welcome with an offer to meet, or even better, invite him or her for a site visit to your organization, whenever it is convenient. Be sure to indicate that you look forward to working with the new program officer and let him or her know that you will be happy to help in any way you can, as he or she steps into the new role. Assume that it will take as much as several months for this individual to be fully up to speed on all aspects relating to your grant project.

If the head of a foundation that has been funding your organization retires or leaves, as a grantee it is appropriate to send a personal note before he or she departs, citing the importance of the foundation's support and praising the good work of your program officer. Be sure to send a copy to your program officer. The letter should go out over the signature of your organization's CEO or chairman of your board. When a new head of the foundation comes in, send a brief welcoming note as a colleague from an organization the foundation supports. Again, the CEO or board chair should sign the letter.

Q. What if a foundation changes its priorities in the middle of your grant, and it appears that your organization will no longer fit the foundation's new guidelines?

A. This is a more common occurrence than you might think. Today's foundation board members are holding their program staff more strictly accountable than ever, requiring them to demonstrate the effectiveness of their grantmaking strategies. A foundation may be in a "holding pattern" while it reassesses its programmatic focus or when a new CEO comes in. Or it may conduct its own strategic assessment and come out of this process with new or different priorities. In a challenging economy some foundations, especially those that have had significant losses in the value of their assets or endowment, may severely restrict their funding or reduce the numbers of grants or the amounts they award. Some have rules about how often and at what time intervals a grantee can return for repeat funding. In tough financial times, on the other hand, some may only be supporting current grantees. Since you already are one, this might actually prove beneficial for you.

It behooves you as a grantee to be very much aware of potential changes in direction at all of the foundations that fund you. It's critical to be on top of these matters well in advance of the normal time you'd be requesting additional funds, so that you can plan accordingly. There may, however, be instances where there is absolutely nothing you can do to change the funder's mind. If you are now truly "outside their guidelines," your program officer may be sympathetic, but his or her hands may be tied. Sometimes the foundation will give you one more "transitional" grant to allow you to find alternate funding. Or your program officer may have suggestions as to other funders that might now be a better fit. Don't expect that you can "talk them out of it," however. That is very unlikely to happen. While it's appropriate to express your disappointment, demonstrating anger in any way will only prove self-defeating in the end.

If a foundation wants to change their program, you must be respectful. Ask them, "Can you help me find other resources?"

  —David Bergholz, Trustee, Cuyahoga Arts and Culture, Cleveland

We're not a bank, after all. We have the unique ability to look at issues from both analytical and qualitative perspectives.

  — Janet Sarbaugh, Senior Director, Heinz Endowments, Pittsburgh, PA

Q. What if a foundation requires particular publicity or other recognition?

A. Your proposal, especially one to a corporate funder, should have included specifics as to your organization's policy on crediting sources of funding. The grant award letter should also contain a written accounting of the foundation's expectations as to recognition, and should have been read carefully at the time you received it. If confusion emerges after the grant project has begun (e.g., they expect their name up in lights, and you had really planned very little or no publicity), you need to clarify expectations immediately.

You should remind the program officer in a warm and courteous manner about what was in the original proposal. As the representative of a corporate foundation or certain other funder types, your program officer may be under a lot of pressure to deliver visibility in return for the grant. Try to come up with a compromise while keeping your own policies firmly in mind. If, for instance, a full press conference is not appropriate, what about a photo release with your leadership and the funding representative? You could disseminate that to the press with a headline and caption that may enhance its chances of actually finding its way into print.

Likewise, if it emerges that the foundation desires credit or a very high level of recognition (like a building or other space named after the founder), talk to your program officer about what level of funding would deserve that naming opportunity. It's possible the funder may want to increase its funding. Or your organization may decide to be flexible in accepting a commitment for a multi-year grant ultimately aimed at reaching the total amount necessary to meet your policy on naming. Again, had you been explicit in your original proposal and/or read the grant award letter carefully, this situation really should not arise. Unfortunately, it sometimes does.

The best advice is to try to position yourself as an honest broker between the needs and desires of your organization and those of the grantmaker.

We set our credit policy up front. It is very clear and adopted by our volunteer leadership. This is key—the formal backing of the volunteer leadership.

  —Shirley Contino-Phillips, Vice President of External Affairs, Westchester
  Community College Foundation, Valhalla, New York

Q. What if a "personality conflict" or serious miscommunication arises between your foundation program officer and you or another staff member at your organization?

A. We're all human. While relatively uncommon, these kind of interpersonal difficulties do crop up. If you experience anger or a negative reaction of any sort on the part of your program officer at any time during the course of the grant, take steps immediately to gain clarity about the nature of the problem. Persist until you are absolutely clear about what is behind your program officer's distress. If it's a question of non-matching expectations, refer back to the original proposal and the grant award letter, but do so in a non-confrontational way.

If this direct approach by phone or mail fails to resolve the issue, ask for a face-to-face meeting or phone conference. And don't delay. Then think about who would best represent your organization at the meeting with an unhappy foundation officer. The highest level person from your organization who can still talk knowledgeably about the grant project is your best bet. The key is to work toward a respectful, collegial discussion resulting in a shared consensus. This may mean that you are not even in the room or on the call. And that's fine. It's not your objective to come out as the "winner" from this confrontation. It's your job as the grantee to ensure a positive relationship moving forward.

It may be helpful to remind yourself that your organization's goals and those of the foundation almost always coincide. And foundations rarely want their grant funds returned. They, as much as you, will want to put the relationship back on an even keel.

Sometimes I see grantseekers trying to figure out the "right formula." This cannot work. Foundations are as diverse as nonprofits and "one-size-fits-all" solutions are seldom successful… Fundamentally this is people making a difference with other people.
—Leonard Aube, Managing Director, Annenberg Foundation, Los Angeles

Q. What if a foundation's grant to your organization requires that you exclude support from another foundation or funding source?

A. Corporate donors are most likely to have these requirements. They may want exclusive credit for the grant project. They may want to hear up front that you are not applying to and will not accept funds from their competitors. This is particularly common when it comes to funds awarded as sponsorships of events. You may be willing to accommodate the funder, if the grant award is at a high enough level. That is a decision for your CEO and/or board. Some private foundations, as well, have policies that preclude their support of organizations that also accept any type of government funding and will want you to verify that you do not.

Once again, all of this should have been clarified long before you begin spending the grant funds. But if these kinds of situations arise during the grant period, you need to be thoughtful. Ask your corporate funding representative if it's okay to apply that funder's funds to particular aspects of the project (with appropriate credit, of course), while others may fund other aspects. Be sure to give your funding representative the opportunity not only to approve the credit to be received in return for his or her support, but also to see the list of others supporting the same project. There should be no surprises at the end of the grant!

If a funder requires that you exclude other donors or categories of donors, let that funder know the circumstances under which your organization is willing to give credit as a sole supporter. Generally this requires a larger grant or an extremely delimited project. These are both options you can consider. Under no circumstances should you attempt to circumvent a funder's policies on these matters. First of all, you are sure to get caught, and secondly, it is very bad practice and will damage your reputation as a grantee, perhaps permanently.

Q. Are there any circumstances under which you should decline a grant award?

A. This is quite rare, but has been known to happen. A funder may surprise you by attaching requirements to a grant that make its acceptance questionable for your organization. The foundation might ask for particular procedures, such as an outside evaluation, collaboration with some other organization, or use of a certain consultant, all matters that were not part of the original proposal or budget. The funder might ask for you to focus on a different constituency or adjust your time frame or utilize materials that really don't fit your plan or coincide with the mission of your organization. As noted earlier, the funder may expect certain forms of recognition, publicity, or issuance of a publication or report that you are unable to deliver. A foundation might give you the grant in the form of a challenge with expectations that you are unlikely to meet, such as raising a very large amount of money in a relatively short period of time in order to satisfy the requirements.

When this happens, your executive director should convene all stakeholders at your organization, including relevant program and finance staff and possibly a special meeting of your board, to determine the parameters of your response. Can your organization meet the foundation's requirements? Do you think accepting this grant is a good way to serve your constituency? In grantmaker relations it is very important to avoid what is called "mission drift" by chasing the grant money rather than doing what you set out to do.

It is possible that minor negotiations with the funder, which could even be done by phone, will enable you to achieve mutually acceptable terms. Perhaps a modest amount of additional funds added to the grant amount will enable you to accomplish what the funder wants, while still fulfilling your own objectives. If there is a larger issue on the table, however, you will probably want to arrange for a face-to-face meeting with your program officer. In either case, if mutually acceptable terms are arrived at, be sure to have the revised grant language in writing.

If, on the other hand, it is not possible to find a mutually acceptable solution, be sure to graciously thank the foundation for considering your organization, and if at all possible leave the door open for working together in the future. The decision not to accept the grant is an institutional one, and is not personal. The key is to walk away with a respectful, shared understanding on the part of both parties involved. In the long run, chances of a successful future relationship are much improved.

Whenever there's a difference between what I think and what the people in the community think, the director is kind of torn. Should they do what the community wants them to do, or should they just do what I want them to do? And the secret is—they have to give a little bit both ways.
      —"Working With Start-Ups," GrantCraft: Practical Wisdom for Grantmakers, A Project of the Ford Foundation[1]

Special circumstances

Q. What if the grant project has unintended negative consequences and/or your organization receives less than flattering media coverage?

A. Assuming the negative press has some validity, it is critical to report to the funder not only on what happened, and how it differed from what was planned, but what was learned as a result. Then you should indicate, based on what was learned, what changes your organization intends to implement moving forward. Most foundation program officers are savvy enough to know that "things happen." The best-constructed grant projects can go awry, sometimes due to circumstances beyond anybody's control. Once again, honesty is paramount when confronting these situations. Your foundation program officer will want to know that your organization is proactive and that it evaluates impact as it goes along and responds to what it learns. Reporting on what didn't work as well as what was planned, and what you are going to do about it, builds trust and respect between your organization and the foundation.

Even in our private-sector partnerships, this is the model. Anything worth doing, and doing well, requires that you understand what you are likely to accomplish and that there are realistic expectations of each partner at the outset. And then you need an agreement on how to measure and monitor performance and adjust over time. You need to ask yourself: what will it take to actually get the job done?
      —Stanley Litow, President, IBM International Foundation, Armonk, New York

---

[1] "Working with Start-Ups: Grant Makers and New Organizations." GrantCraft. *GrantCraft.*: Practical Wisdom for Grantmakers, 2004. (www.grantcraft.org/dl_pdf/startups.pdf).

Q. What if a scandal erupts involving your organization?

A. One thing worse than the scandal itself is having your funder learn about it via the press or word of mouth. In the case of any type of scandal, no matter how seemingly inconsequential, you must communicate with all funders personally and immediately. Some organizations, especially those involved in controversial program areas or almost any form of advocacy, have a crisis intervention plan and a standing emergency response team ready to be implemented when the need arises. The plan and the team can be deployed with less than a day's notice.

Hopefully, a true scandal involving your organization will never happen. But in case it does, it is critical to have your response to the media and to your funders carefully reviewed by your attorney, and if money is involved, by your auditors, as quickly as is feasible. When talking with funders about a scandal, develop a script that your staff is expected to strictly adhere to. Be sure to contact each and every funder (most likely by telephone). You want to get there first, before they hear about the problem elsewhere. The script very narrowly defines the problem and what is being done to address it. It doesn't seek to solve the problem instantaneously. However, some response may already be underway and you will want to share what that is. Here are a few examples of immediate responses to a developing scandal: An individual may be put on leave until an investigation is complete. A new audit may be underway. A facility may be closed until safety issues can be assessed. Operations of a clinic or daycare center may be suspended until a flu or other epidemic passes.

Don't try to sweep what is happening under the rug. And above all, in terms of your relationship with your funder, be sure to address what is happening specifically to the foundation's funded project. In all but the most extreme instances, you should be able to reassure your funder that, no matter what, the funder will be held harmless.

In the case of a scandal, identify in advance who could help you. Who will take the calls at your institution? Get professional advice. Be honest and up front. There is very little that cannot be worked out.
        —Jane Safer, Cultural Consultant, New York

Q. What if your funder is caught up in a scandal?

A. Although it is unusual for nonprofits, including foundations, to be caught up in a scandal, it does happen from time to time. You should have a point person (usually the CEO) who represents your organization. Ideally this individual will have been coached by a public relations professional to handle calls from the press on any negative issue arising concerning a source of your organization's funding. Generally your response will entail an expression of concern about the news, followed by an immediate indication of how sorry you were to hear about it. Then the conversation moves as quickly as possible to the good work that the foundation's grant has supported and your worry about the constituency you serve.

In extreme circumstances a judge may order a forensic audit of the grantees of a scandal-plagued foundation. This is done to ascertain whether grantees were also part of the fraud under investigation. Be sure that your own auditor is aware and take his or her advice, just as you would if a foundation chose to audit you in the course of its own due diligence with its grantees.

Q. What if your funder moves beyond its appropriate behind-the-scenes role and takes steps that seem to involve it in the actual design or management of your programs?

A. This issue typically presents itself prior to the actual grant award and may come up during the proposal submission and review period. We speak often of becoming partners with our funders, and some may view this partnership as actually helping run your project or organization. How much funder involvement your organization is willing to tolerate is a decision for your CEO and board. But distinct boundaries and what constitutes overstepping them should be absolutely clear to both sides well before the grant project commences. You need to know whether or not you will be operating as though the grant were actually more of a contract fulfilling work for the foundation.

You have a choice. If the foundation's expectations about its level of involvement sound too much like interference, you can always decline the offer of funding and move on to solicit another foundation for your program. The same is true in terms of seeking renewal funding. Working with some funders may simply not be worth it in terms of maintaining your organization's autonomy. Sometimes we want the grant money so badly that we prefer to overlook clear signals from the funder. But it is naive to think that a foundation program officer who makes unreasonable demands prior to the grant award will suddenly become a more flexible colleague after the grant is made.

Evaluate and decide on your own. But don't chase the money.
—David Bergholz, Trustee, Cuyahoga Arts & Culture, Cleveland

Q. What if you encounter serious obstacles with the grant project, which are so substantial that it must change significantly in scope, or it will fail completely? What if these changes go even further and impact your entire organization?

A. Often, especially in a challenging economy, these kinds of big changes have to do with funding shortfalls. If it comes to pass for one reason or another (e.g., an anticipated grant or government contract falls through, an expected major gift from an individual fails to materialize), and you simply don't have the funds to do what you said you would do in your original proposal, there are still steps you can take, in concert with your foundation program officer, of course. As we've stated previously, the last thing the foundation wants is for you to have to return the grant funds.

One option is for your project or operations to simply shrink in size or scope. You might reduce or more narrowly define the constituency you serve. Or you may continue to serve a large constituency but with diluted services. An example is maintaining all the seniors for daily lunch at a community center, but eliminating the health, cultural, and/or social services they formerly received as part of the program. In other words, you are focusing on your core services and at least temporarily eliminating the "extras."

Another kind of change might happen because you lost a required operating license, lost your lease or use of space, or lost an affiliation that was necessary in order for you to deliver your services. In these instances your CEO and board need to put their heads together to come up with some workable solution that will satisfy the funder and still respond to the intent if not the exact letter of the original grant award.

A final category of dramatic change often befalls organizations whose grant projects are blazing new trails, in the fields of medical research or social justice, or bringing together people or groups that do not traditionally work together, opening up corrupt or highly bureaucratic structures, or organizing very disparate people around a common cause. Presumably the fact that these kinds of grant projects carry greater risk of potential midstream adjustment, or even of partial failure, was obvious to the funder from the get-go. It is likely that only a foundation with a higher than usual tolerance for risk would be attracted to such projects in the first place. Nonetheless, critical under these circumstances is frequent and frank communication with your funding representative and making sure this happens before the situation deteriorates to the point where the grant project is irrevocably damaged.

If goals and objectives are clear as are the methods of measurement in the proposal and grant award letter (and fully understood among the participants), then adjustments can of course be made, dependent on external and internal barriers or events, juxtaposed against the available resources. Revision in tactics and strategies then becomes more of a collaboration or real partnership.
—Stanley Litow, President, IBM International Foundation, New York

In these circumstances, you must reach out to your funding base. Share your situation and your plans for action. Be frank. Be honest. Then a foundation can choose to help or guide you to others who can help. Part of the role of a program officer is to engage in this kind of problem solving.
—Michelle Boone, Program Officer, The Joyce Foundation, Chicago

To sum up, even in the worst-case scenario, it is always best to have a frank and open relationship with your foundation representative before anything the least bit controversial arises. So begin now, just in case, to cultivate your donor. This includes faithfully communicating anecdotes that spell success, sharing special quotes from satisfied constituents, and informing the funder of recognition received by the organization or its staff. Try to aim for a note or e-mail or voice message every quarter, or more frequently if warranted. Then, when difficulties arise, you will be communicating with a friend and colleague and not, for the very first time, a standoffish program officer who barely knows you or your organization. That will make all the difference.

Appendix B—Author Biographies

Debbie Rosenberg Bush

Debbie Rosenberg Bush is senior director of development at the Cancer Support Community, likely the largest professionally led network of cancer support worldwide, and formed by the combination of Gilda's Club and the Wellness Community. She was previously director of corporate and foundation relations at Gilda's Club Worldwide, and served as director of foundation support at the American Museum of Natural History and director of development at the New York Academy of Sciences. Before her career in development, Debbie spent many years at Memorial Sloan-Kettering Cancer Center as director of publications in the Department of Public Affairs. She has also served as an editor of various publications for Random House and Consumer Reports. Debbie is a member of the Association of Fundraising Professionals and Women in Development New York and serves on the board of the Yale Alumni Fund.

Diane Carillo

Diane Carillo joined the National Park Foundation as director of foundation relations in July 2008. She has held positions in foundation fundraising with the American Museum of Natural History, Pratt Institute, and Scenic Hudson. A former English teacher and planner/director in a New York City company, Ms. Carillo has worked in nonprofit development and marketing for the last fifteen years, including positions as advancement officer at the Community Foundation of Jackson Hole and marketing director at the Teton Science School. Ms. Carillo holds a BA in English and secondary education from the State University of New York at New Paltz and a masters in cinema studies from New York University.

Eleanor Cicerchi

Eleanor Cicerchi has extensive experience in fundraising management and consulting for museums, international humanitarian organizations, colleges, and health care organizations. She is also a frequent speaker and writer about fundraising and nonprofit management. Since September 2007, she has served as director of the Signature Campaign for the Newark Museum in Newark, NJ. Previously she was director of development for the Corning Museum of Glass in Corning, NY; associate vice president for development for Save the Children, an international child-assistance agency; vice president for development and external affairs/Americas for ORBIS International, a global blindness-prevention agency; and chief development officer for amfAR, the American Foundation for AIDS Research. She also served as a campaign director for Brakeley, John Price Jones Inc., and, in that capacity, directed the Foundation Center's first capital campaign.

Ms. Cicerchi is a faculty member in the nonprofit management graduate program of the New School University as well as the Fund Raising School of the Center on Philanthropy at Indiana University. She has also been an adjunct faculty member in NYU's master's program in visual arts management. In 2004 she was named Professional Fund Raiser of the Year by the Ithaca, New York–based chapter of the Association of Fund Raising Professionals. A graduate of Mount Holyoke College and a Woodrow Wilson Fellow, she has a master's in nonprofit management from The New School University and has earned the Certified Fund-Raising Executive (CFRE) designation from the Association of Fund Raising Professionals. A current or former board member of a variety of nonprofits, she is the immediate past chair and current executive board member of the Development & Membership Committee for the American Association of Museums and a board member of Beckoning for Change in NYC and ActionAID International USA, which works to end poverty in the developing world.

Elan DiMaio

Elan DiMaio, a graduate of Princeton University, is currently a student at University of Pennsylvania Law School. For two years she served as Planning and Evaluation Fellow at the Foundation Center, in which capacity she was assistant editor of *After the Grant* and responsible for integration of grantmaker interviews, quotes, and sample documents, as well as selection and composition of the case studies.

Sidney Hargro

Sidney Hargro has been with the Columbus Foundation since May 2000. Starting as a program officer, his duties were expanded in 2003 when he managed the foundation's investigation of community knowledge management practices starting with an organization-wide knowledge audit. In 2005, he was the project manager for development of The Columbus Foundation's business strategy along with the president and CEO and two board members—a project that identified community knowledge management as the chief value proposition that the foundation offered to existing and prospective donors. As a result, community knowledge development and sharing became one of seven (now nine) prioritized measures used to rate the foundation's annual performance, raising the importance of information capital to the level of financial capital.

In 2007, Mr. Hargro became the senior officer for strategy and organizational learning, and his first project was managing a radical redesign of the foundation's web site with PowerPhilanthropy, a nonprofit knowledge base powered by DonorEdge, as the cornerstone. The new web site officially ushered in the foundation's commitment to integrating community knowledge and social media into the work of the foundation. Currently, Mr. Hargro manages activities associated with the foundation's social impact evaluation; cross-departmental innovation strategy; business strategy and organizational performance measures; and grantmaking.

John Hicks

John Hicks, CFRE, joined J.C. Geever, Inc. in 1988 and became president and CEO upon the firm's 25th anniversary in 2000. He provides consultation and strategic guidance for annual and capital fundraising programs for a variety of clients ranging from grassroots to national nonprofit organizations. Mr. Hicks is a contributing author to John Wiley and Sons' *Fund Raising Handbook* (2001 edition) and has published articles in *Fund Raising Management* and *Advancing Philanthropy*. He currently serves on the faculty of Columbia University's Master of Science in Fundraising Management program. A member of the Association of Fundraising Professionals, he is currently president of the Greater New York Chapter of AFP, and has both chaired and served as a member of several International AFP task forces. In 2003 and 2004, he served as chair of Fund Raising Day in New York, the nation's largest one-day conference on philanthropy. He is a past member of the board of the AAFRC Trust for Philanthropy. Mr. Hicks holds degrees from the University of North Carolina at Chapel Hill and the University of Hartford.

Marilyn Hoyt

Based in Chicago and New York, Marilyn Hoyt consults nationally. She serves on the Steering Committee of the National Public Housing Museum in Chicago and is an Advisory Board member of the Columbia University Masters in Fund Raising program as well as the Louis Latimer House Museum in New York City. She is a member of the national Young Audiences Program Certification Team and serves as a reviewer for a major mid-west arts-funding foundation. Volunteer efforts include work with the Rutgers Center for Nonprofit and Philanthropic Leadership, Fund Raising Day in New York, and the Norwalk Aquarium in Connecticut.

Over the last 40 years Ms. Hoyt's work included 12 years in cultural grantmaking in Washington and New York; fundraising consulting with J.C. Geever, Inc. serving clients in New York, New Jersey, and California; and 20 years in advancement and as the founding CEO of the New York Hall of Science. There she led the raising of nearly $200 million from corporations, foundations, government, and individuals, including a $92 million capital campaign, doubling the Hall. She recently authored the fundraising chapter for the *Handbook for Small Science Centers* and articles on outsourcing during tough economic times for the Association of Science-Technology Centers.

Victoria Kovar

Victoria Kovar has worked for the Cooper Foundation in Lincoln, Nebraska, for 15 years. As Program Officer she manages the grantmaking activities for the foundation and enjoys working with nonprofits and helping them craft their best proposals. Ms. Kovar has served on boards of various nonprofit and community organizations and is especially interested in the arts and community development. She studied English and art at the University of Nebraska-Lincoln and is pursuing a Master of Public Administration degree at the University of Nebraska at Omaha. As member of the Council on Foundations, Foundation Center, the Grants Managers Network, and a local funders group, the Cooper Foundation shares information and expertise with the goal of following and promoting best practices in grant making.

Jane B. O'Connell

Jane B. O'Connell is president of the Altman Foundation, a $220 million foundation established in 1913 under the will of Benjamin Altman. The foundation funds in the areas of education, health, strengthening communities, and the arts, with a focus on initiatives that help individuals, families, and communities benefit from services and opportunities that will enable them to achieve their full potential. She also consults for schools and small nonprofit organizations in the areas of nonprofit management, fundraising, strategic planning, and board development. From 1976 to 1998, Ms. O'Connell worked at the Convent of the Sacred Heart, an independent school in New York City, in various roles including director of development and administrative affairs, treasurer, and chief financial officer and was responsible for strategic planning.

Ms. O'Connell began her professional career as an English teacher in a New York City public high school. She is a trustee of the Lavelle Fund for the Blind and the Endowment for Inner-City Education, where she chairs the disbursement committee. She serves on the board of Early Steps, a program that assists minority families in admission to independent schools. She is a member of the national board of Grantmakers for Children Youth and Families and is on the advisory board for the Fundraising Management Master of Science Program at Columbia University. She is a trustee and treasurer of the Museum of the City of New York and is a member of the board of Volunteer Consulting Group. Previous board work includes the Association of Fundraising Professionals, New York Chapter; Governance Matters; and City Harvest. She is a frequent presenter at workshops on nonprofit management and fundraising. Ms. O'Connell is a graduate of Manhattanville College and received her M.A. in secondary education from New York University (Steinhardt) School of Education.

Stephanie Rapp

Stephanie Rapp has 26 years of experience in nonprofit management and organizational development. She has been a senior program officer at the Walter and Elise Haas Fund since 2003 and currently co-chairs the Disaster Preparedness and Response Committee of Northern California Grantmakers. She served as executive director of the United Nations Association for four years, and, later, as director of the UN50 Committee, charged with planning and coordinating the commemoration of the 50th anniversary of the signing of the UN Charter in San Francisco. She served as special assistant to the secretary general of Habitat, the UN's agency in charge of housing and urbanization, and coordinated events for the secretary general at the City Summit in Istanbul. She has held numerous positions in nonprofit organizations, including director of development for both the San Francisco Education Fund and the World Affairs Council of Northern California.

Michael Seltzer

Michael Seltzer is a partner at Rabin Strategic Partners, where he is responsible for the firm's philanthropic services practice. He has worked in the nonprofit sector for more than forty years, including serving as the president of the New York Regional Association of Grantmakers and the program officer responsible for strengthening the nonprofit sector and advancing organized philanthropy at the Ford Foundation. His commentaries appear regularly on PhilanTopic, the blog of the Foundation Center. He is the author of *Securing Your Organization's Future*.

Nancy Wiltsek

Nancy Wiltsek has more than 25 years of experience in the nonprofit sector working with individuals, foundations, and corporate giving programs as well as nonprofit management and training organizations in various capacities. Currently a philanthropic consultant, she served as executive director of the Pottruck Family Foundation in San Francisco from 1999 to 2009. She is a member of the National Network of Consultants to Grantmakers (NNCG) and is a former chair of the Advisory Board of the San Francisco branch of the Foundation Center. In addition she chairs the northern California Grantmakers' Family Philanthropy Exchange Committee and is a trustee of the Gagarin Trust, whose grantmaking focuses on human rights in St. Petersburg, Russia. Ms. Wiltsek holds a master's degree in nonprofit administration from the University of San Francisco and bachelor's degree in anthropology from U.C. Berkeley, and was trained as a retreat facilitator through the Center for Courage and Renewal.

Appendix C—Bibliography

Compiled by Jimmy Tom, Manager of Bibliographic Services
The Foundation Center

Brinckerhoff, Peter C. *Nonprofit Stewardship: A Better Way to Lead Your Mission-Based Organization*. St. Paul, MN: Fieldstone Alliance, 2004.
> Brinckerhoff deliberates on the concept of stewardship in this time of diminishing resources and increasing demand for nonprofit services. In the introductory chapters he explains the philosophy and precepts of stewardship, and then follows up with more detailed ideas as they relate to planning, financial aspects, and unexpected situations.

Brown, Larissa Golden and Martin John Brown. *Demystifying Grant Seeking: What You Really Need to Do to Get Grants*. San Francisco, CA: Jossey-Bass Publishers, 2001.
> This book confronts some common ideas about the fundraising process and offers the building blocks of a systematic grants effort. The chapter "Follow Up After a Funding Decision" includes a form to help you plan and track follow-up activities.

Chait, Richard P., William P. Ryan, and Barbara E. Taylor. *Governance as Leadership: Reframing the Work of Nonprofit Boards*. Hoboken, NJ: John Wiley & Sons, 2005.
> Presents an analytical treatment of three modes of governance and follows with practical initiatives that boards can adopt. The book is directed primarily to trustees and leaders who are concerned with strategic change for their organizations.

Fairfield, Kent D. and Kennard T. Wing. "Collaboration in Foundation Grantor-Grantee Relationships." *Nonprofit Management & Leadership*, vol. 19 (Fall 2008): p. 27–44.
> An exploratory study of the relations between foundations and their grantee organizations, this article notes the traits of productive collaborations and offers suggestions on how to replicate

these cooperative funder-grantee relationships. The authors base their research on a focus group of five nonprofit chief executives and interviews with representatives from eight foundations and eight nonprofits.

Flood, Henry. "Essentials of Grants Management: A Guide for the Perplexed." *Grantsmanship Center Magazine*, vol. 45 (Fall 2001): p. 6–8, 11–2. (Full text available online)
The article outlines twelve core principles for effective grants management, with a focus on requirements for federal grants. Topics covered include task management, compliance, financial management, purchasing systems, personnel practices, property management, audit management, and ethics.

Geever, Jane C. *The Foundation Center's Guide to Proposal Writing*. 5th ed. New York, NY: Foundation Center, 2007.
The work guides the grantwriter from pre-proposal planning to post-grant follow-up. The chapter "Life After the Grant—or Rejection" contains sample thank-you letters, grant agreements, and grant reports.

Hank Rosso's Achieving Excellence in Fund Raising. 2nd ed. San Francisco, CA: Jossey-Bass Publishers, 2003.
The book features comprehensive coverage of successful and ethical fundraising principles, concepts, and techniques. The chapter "Practicing Stewardship" describes the characteristics of good stewardship, including accountability, gratitude, leadership, quality, and justice.

Hedge, Kathy, Eva Nico, and Lindsay Fox. *Advancing Good Governance: How Grantmakers Invest in the Governance of Nonprofit Organizations*. Boston, MA: FSG Social Impact Advisors, 2009.
Based on interviews with representatives from 54 grantmaking institutions, this report develops the case for investing in governance; describes current models and examples; and provides guidance for grantmakers to engage nonprofits on governance issues.

Hedrick, Janet L. *Nonprofit Essentials: Effective Donor Relations*. Hoboken, NJ: John Wiley & Sons, 2008.
This book explains the importance and essential processes of donor recognition and stewardship, with numerous examples throughout the book. These techniques relate largely, but not solely, to individual donors.

Hoekstra, Joel. "When Grantmakers Come Calling." *Grantsmanship Center Magazine*, vol. 38 (Summer 1999): p. 29–30. (Full text available online)
Hoekstra provides eight pointers for preparing for a grantmaker site visit.

Levy, Reynold. *Yours for the Asking: An Indispensable Guide to Fundraising and Management*. Hoboken, NJ: John Wiley & Sons, 2008.
Levy's book covers individual prospects, corporate and foundation fundraising, special events, direct mail, and the role of volunteers, as well as numerous personal anecdotes.

More Than Money: Making a Difference with Assistance Beyond the Grant. Cambridge, MA: Center for Effective Philanthropy, 2008.

> This research report examines what types of support funders can offer in addition to grants, such as advice, training, or collaborations. It looks at the attitudes of grantmakers and grantees toward these types of assistance and also includes several case studies.

Orosz, Joel J. *The Insider's Guide to Grantmaking: How Foundations Find, Fund, and Manage Effective Programs*. San Francisco, CA: Jossey-Bass Publishers, 2000.

> Written primarily for program officers of foundations, the volume contains chapters that discuss issues grantmakers face when managing and closing projects.

Quick, James Aaron and Cheryl Carter New. *Grant Winner's Toolkit: Project Management and Evaluation*. New York, NY: John Wiley & Sons, 2000.

> The volume covers the grantseeking process from planning through evaluation, with chapters that explain how to manage a funded program and develop continuation strategies.

Robinson, Andy. *Grassroots Grants: An Activist's Guide to Grantseeking*. 2nd ed. San Francisco, CA: Jossey-Bass Publishers, 2004.

> Robinson presents a pragmatic look at how foundations function and how grantseeking fits in with an overall fundraising strategy for grassroots activists. The chapter on "Successful Grants Administration" contains tips on record keeping, reporting, managing grant funds, and other topics.

Scanlan, Eugene A. *Corporate and Foundation Fund Raising: A Complete Guide From the Inside*. Frederick, MD: Aspen Publishers, 1997.

> Scanlan provides an overview of the various types of corporate foundations and giving programs, as well as private and community foundations, followed by appropriate techniques for approaching them effectively. The chapter "After the Grant: Maintaining the Relationship" provides guidance on reporting requirements, unanticipated problems, and future funding.

Seltzer, Michael. *Securing Your Organization's Future: A Complete Guide to Fundraising Strategies*. Rev. Ed. New York, NY: Foundation Center, 2001.

> This book is a step-by-step approach to creating and sustaining a network of funding sources and discusses major organizational tasks to address; the world of money available to nonprofits; techniques for approaching both individuals and institutions for support; how to create a funding mix that succeeds; and how to capitalize on the uniqueness of your organization. It also includes case studies, worksheets, and bibliographies with accompanying discussions.

Wason, Sara Deming. *Webster's New World Grant Writing Handbook*. Hoboken, NJ: John Wiley & Sons, 2004.

> Wason covers project planning, funding research, proposal development, and writing. The Chapter "Effective Stewardship" provides advice on recognizing funders and communicating with them.

York, Peter. *A Funder's Guide to Evaluation: Leveraging Evaluation to Improve Nonprofit Effectiveness.* Saint Paul, MN: Fieldstone Alliance, 2005.

    The volume explains how evaluation is a capacity-building tool that promotes a learning partnership between grantmakers and grantees.

Index